# 11+ Non-Verbal Reasoning

# For the **CEM** test

When it comes to the 11+, getting top marks is key — and this CGP Stretch book is packed with extra-tricky questions to help pupils aged 10-11 master the hardest parts of the test.

It starts with a section of challenging questions for each topic, so children can practise each question type. Then, there's a selection of mixed-topic Assessment Tests where they can work on really polishing their exam technique.

We've also included detailed, step-by-step answers. Everything you need!

---

### How to access your free Online Edition

This book includes a free Online Edition to read on your PC, Mac or tablet.
You'll just need to go to **cgpbooks.co.uk/extras** and enter this code:

## 1714 8390 9143 9002

By the way, this code only works for one person. If somebody else has used this book before you, they might have already claimed the Online Edition.

---

# Stretch Practice Book
# Ages 10-11
## with Assessment Tests

# How to use this Practice Book

This book is divided into five parts — 'Similarities and Differences', 'Pairs, Series and Grids', 'Rotation and Reflection', 'Spatial Reasoning', and 'Assessment Tests'. There are answers and detailed explanations at the back of the book.

### 'Similarities and Differences', 'Pairs, Series and Grids' and 'Rotation and Reflection'

- Each section contains the different question types your child will need to be familiar with for the Non-Verbal Reasoning part of the test.

- These pages can help your child build up the different skills they'll need for the real test.

- Particularly hard questions are marked up with an orange box around the question number.

- Your child can use the smiley face tick boxes to evaluate how confident they feel with each type of question.

### Spatial Reasoning

- This part concentrates on the skills your child will need for the 3D and folding questions in the test.

### Assessment Tests

- This part of the book contains three assessment tests, each with a mix of question types.

- You can print multiple-choice answer sheets so your child can practise the tests as if they're sitting the real thing — visit cgpbooks.co.uk/11plus/answer-sheets or scan the QR code.

- Use the printable answer sheets if you want your child to do each test more than once.

- If you want to give your child timed practice, give them a time limit of 45 minutes for each test, and ask them to work as quickly and carefully as they can.

- Talk your child through the answers to the questions they got wrong. This will help them understand questions that work in a similar way when they come up against them again.

- Your child should aim for a mark of around 80% (34 questions correct) in each test. If they score less than this, use their results to work out the areas they need more practice on.

- If they haven't managed to finish the test in time, they should work on increasing their speed, whereas if they have made a lot of mistakes, they may need to work more carefully.

- Keep track of your child's scores using the progress chart on page 74.

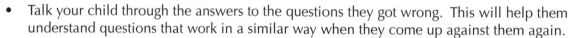

Published by CGP

Editors:
Michael Bushell, Alex Fairer, Katherine Faudemer

With thanks to Sharon Keeley-Holden and Glenn Rogers for the proofreading.

ISBN: 978 1 78908 982 0
Printed by Elanders Ltd, Newcastle upon Tyne
Clipart from Corel®

Based on the classic CGP style created by Richard Parsons.

Text, design, layout and original illustrations © Coordination Group Publications Ltd. (CGP) 2022 All rights reserved.

# Contents

# Odd One Out

Find the figure in each row that is most unlike the other figures.

Example:

    **a**          **b**          **c**          **d**          **e**    ( _a_ )

In all other figures, the hatching in the square is going diagonally down to the right.

1.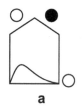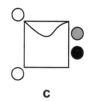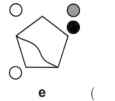

    **a**          **b**          **c**          **d**          **e**    ( ___ )

2.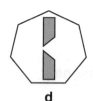

    **a**          **b**          **c**          **d**          **e**    ( ___ )

3.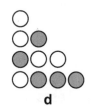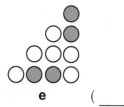

    **a**          **b**          **c**          **d**          **e**    ( ___ )

4.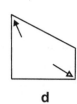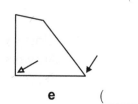

    **a**          **b**          **c**          **d**          **e**    ( ___ )

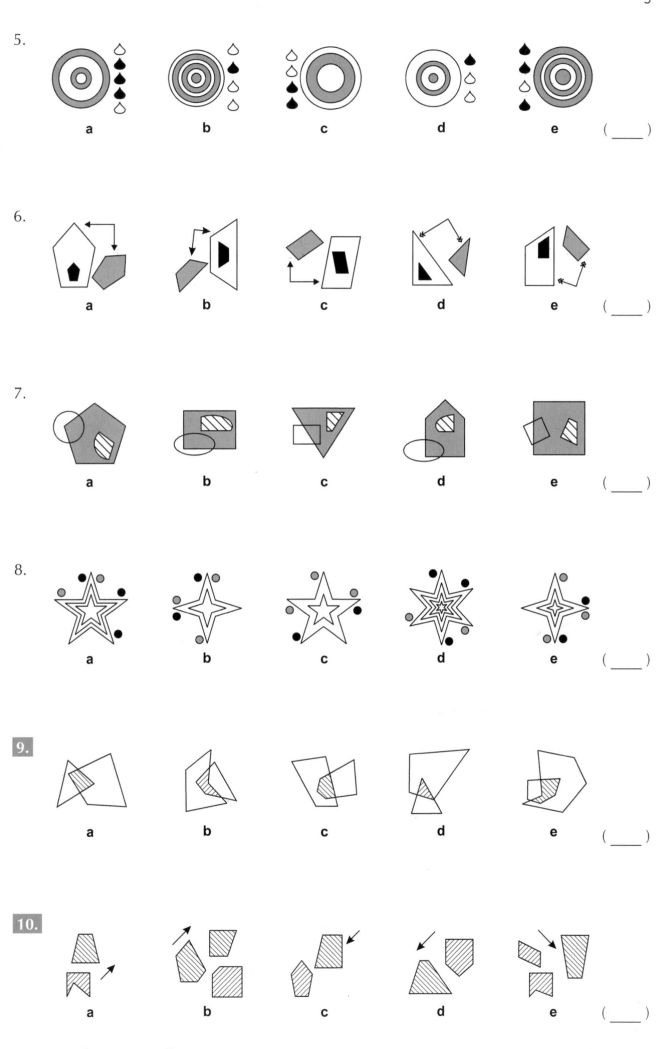

5.

   a        b        c        d        e    (    )

6.

   a        b        c        d        e    (    )

7.

   a        b        c        d        e    (    )

8.

   a        b        c        d        e    (    )

9.

   a        b        c        d        e    (    )

10.

   a        b        c        d        e    (    )

# Find the Figure Like the First Two or Three

Work out which option is most like the two figures on the left.

Example:

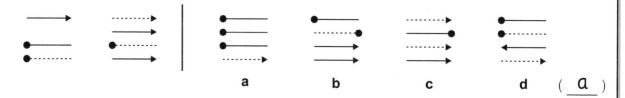

( __a__ )

In all figures, arrows with a circular arrowhead must point left and arrows with a triangular arrowhead must point right.

Work out which option is most like the three figures on the left.

Example:

a       b       c       d       ( __C__ )

In all figures, the shapes are arranged in order of increasing number of sides, from top to bottom.

1.

a       b       c       d       ( ____ )

2.

a       b       c       d       ( ____ )

3.

a       b       c       d       ( ____ )

Similarities and Differences

4.

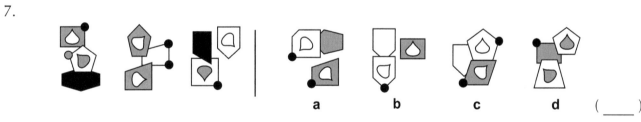

( _____ )

5.

( _____ )

6.

( _____ )

7.

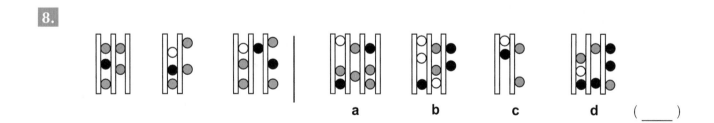

( _____ )

8.

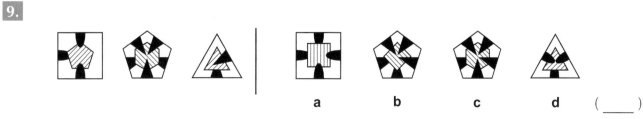

( _____ )

9.

a      b      c      d

( _____ )

# Complete the Pair

Look at how the first two figures are changed, and then work out which option would look like the third figure if you changed it in the same way.

Example:

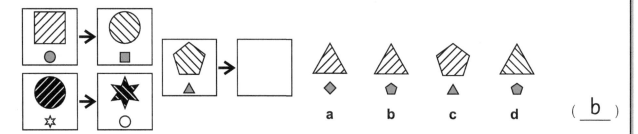

( _b_ )

The two shapes swap position, size and shading.  The hatching reflects across.

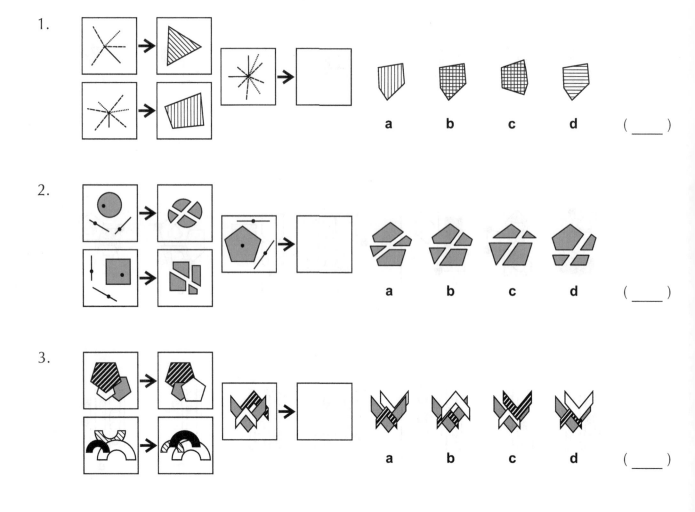

5.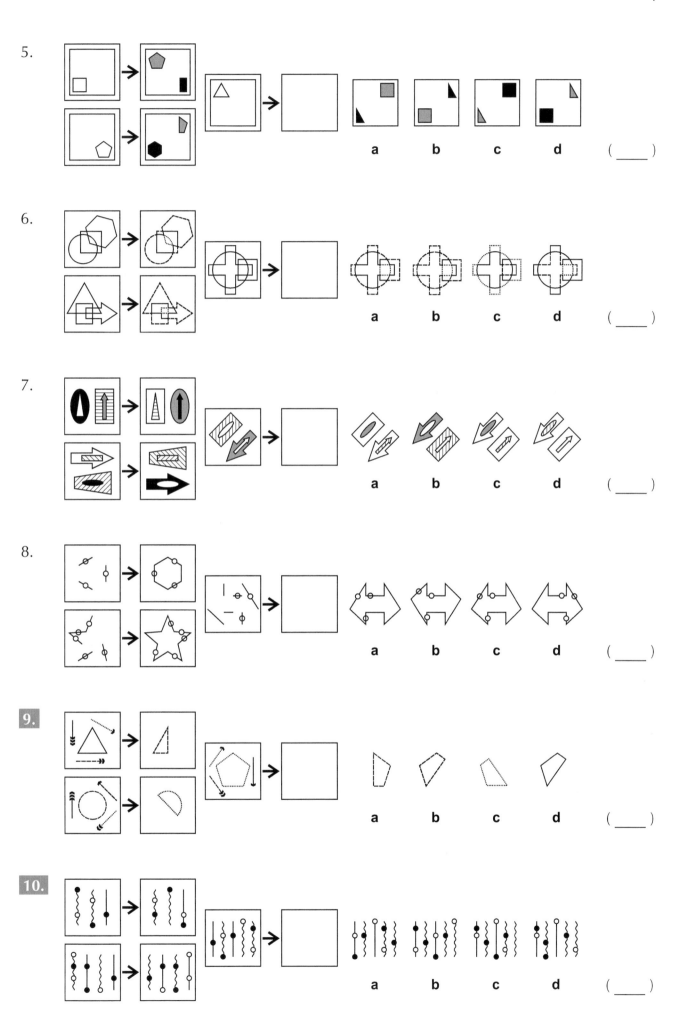

6.

7.

8.

9.

10.

# Complete the Series

Work out which of the options best fits in place of the missing square in the series.

Example:

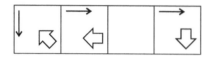    

            **a**        **b**        **c**        **d**    ( _b_ )

The arrow-style line swaps direction and the white arrow rotates 45 degrees anticlockwise in each series square.

1.

            **a**        **b**        **c**        **d**    ( ___ )

2.

            **a**        **b**        **c**        **d**    ( ___ )

3.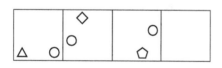

            **a**        **b**        **c**        **d**    ( ___ )

4.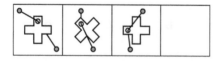

            **a**        **b**        **c**        **d**    ( ___ )

5.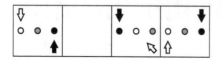

            **a**        **b**        **c**        **d**    ( ___ )

6.

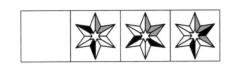    

                                           **a**        **b**        **c**        **d**      ( \_\_\_ )

7.

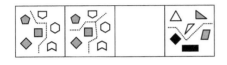    

                                           **a**        **b**        **c**        **d**      ( \_\_\_ )

8.

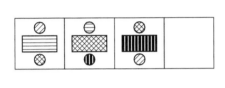    

                                           **a**        **b**        **c**        **d**      ( \_\_\_ )

9.

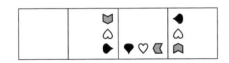    

                                           **a**        **b**        **c**        **d**      ( \_\_\_ )

10.

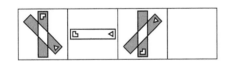    

                                           **a**        **b**        **c**        **d**      ( \_\_\_ )

**11.**

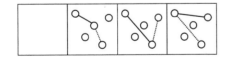    

                                           **a**        **b**        **c**        **d**      ( \_\_\_ )

**12.**

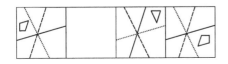    

                                           **a**        **b**        **c**        **d**      ( \_\_\_ )

# Complete the Square Grid

Work out which of the options best fits in place of the missing square in the grid.
Example:

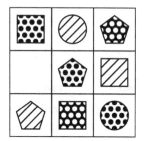 

a    b    c    d

( _b_ )

Each shape and each type of shading appears once in each row and column.

1.

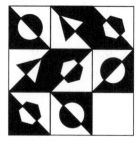

a    b    c    d    ( ___ )

2.

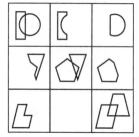

a    b    c    d    ( ___ )

3.

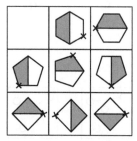

a    b    c    d    ( ___ )

4.

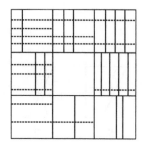

a    b    c    d    ( ___ )

Pairs, Series and Grids

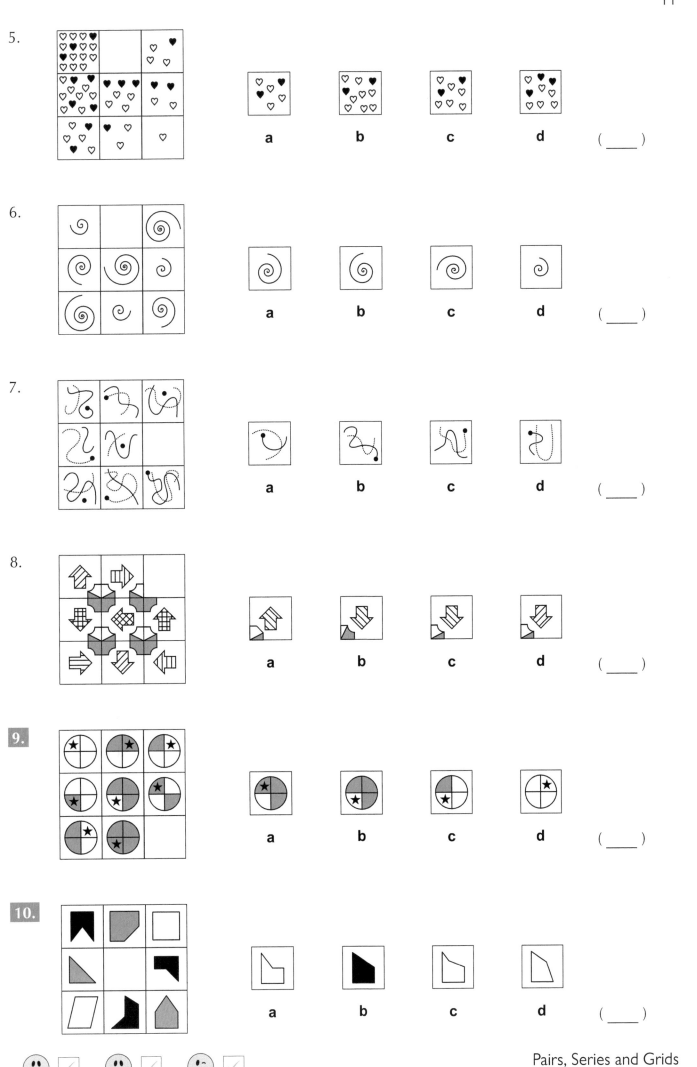

# Complete the Hexagonal Grid

Work out which of the options best fits in place of the missing hexagon in the grid.

Example:

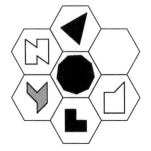    

a      b      c      d      ( **a** )

Going in a clockwise direction from the top hexagon, the number of sides of the shape increases by one in each grid square. The shading changes from black to grey to white and then starts from black again.

1.

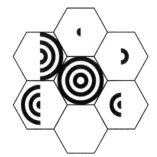

a      b      c      d      ( ___ )

2.

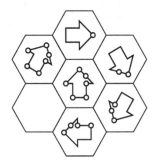   

a      b      c      d      ( ___ )

3.

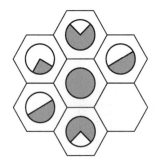   

a      b      c      d      ( ___ )

4.

a       b       c       d       ( ____ )

5.

a       b       c       d       ( ____ )

6.

a       b       c       d       ( ____ )

7.

a       b       c       d       ( ____ )

8.

a       b       c       d       ( ____ )

Pairs, Series and Grids

# Changing Bugs

Look at how the first bug changes to become the second bug. Then work out which option would look like the third bug if you changed it in the same way.

Example:

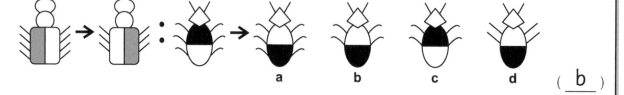

a      b      c      d      ( b )

The bug loses a leg from each side. The shadings inside the bug's body swap.

1.

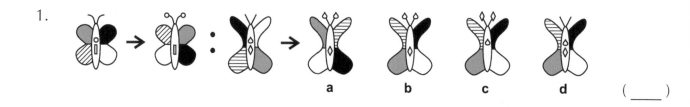

a      b      c      d      ( ___ )

2.

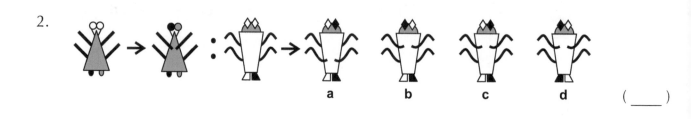

a      b      c      d      ( ___ )

3.

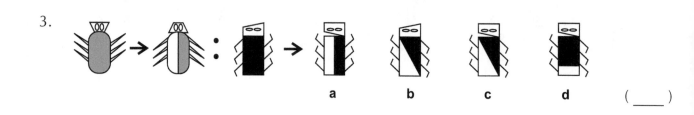

a      b      c      d      ( ___ )

4.

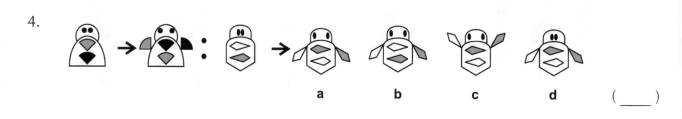

a      b      c      d      ( ___ )

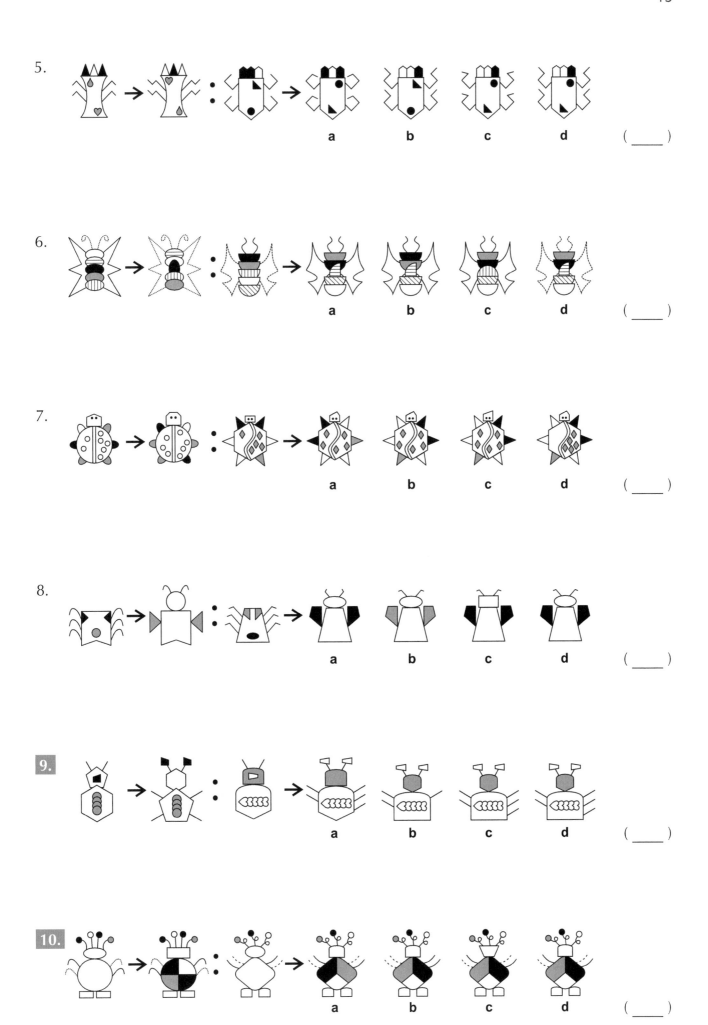

5.  ( _____ )

6.  ( _____ )

7.  ( _____ )

8.  ( _____ )

9.  ( _____ )

10. ( _____ )

Pairs, Series and Grids

# Rotate the Figure

Work out which option would look like the figure on the left if it was rotated.

Example:

**Rotate**

           **a**           **b**           **c**           **d**     ( **b** )

The figure has been rotated 90 degrees anticlockwise.

1.

**Rotate**

           **a**           **b**           **c**           **d**     (     )

2.

**Rotate**

           **a**           **b**           **c**           **d**     (     )

3.

**Rotate**

           **a**           **b**           **c**           **d**     (     )

4.

**Rotate**

           **a**           **b**           **c**           **d**     (     )

5.

**Rotate**

a     b     c     d     ( _____ )

6.

**Rotate**

a     b     c     d     ( _____ )

7.

**Rotate**

a     b     c     d     ( _____ )

8.

**Rotate**

a     b     c     d     ( _____ )

9.

**Rotate**

a     b     c     d     ( _____ )

10.

**Rotate**

a     b     c     d     ( _____ )

Rotation and Reflection

# Reflect the Figure

Work out which option would look like the figure on the left if it was reflected over the line.

Example:

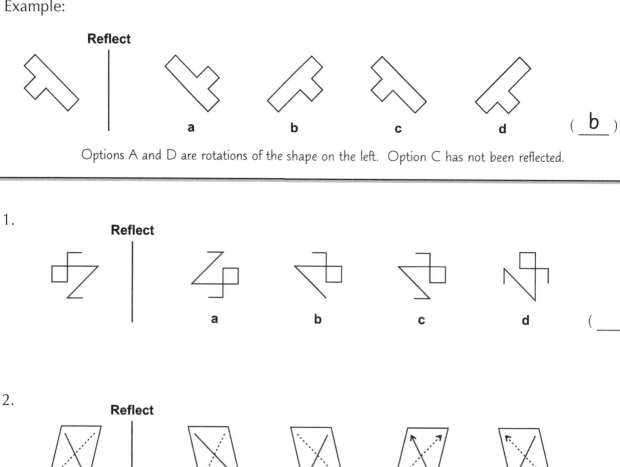

**Reflect**

a     b     c     d     ( _b_ )

Options A and D are rotations of the shape on the left. Option C has not been reflected.

1.

**Reflect**

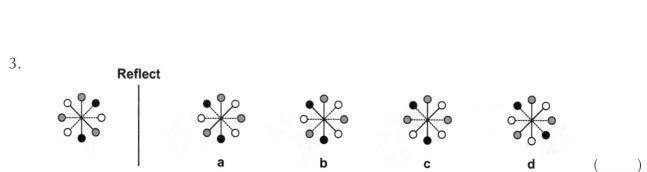

a     b     c     d     ( ___ )

2.

**Reflect**

a     b     c     d     ( ___ )

3.

**Reflect**

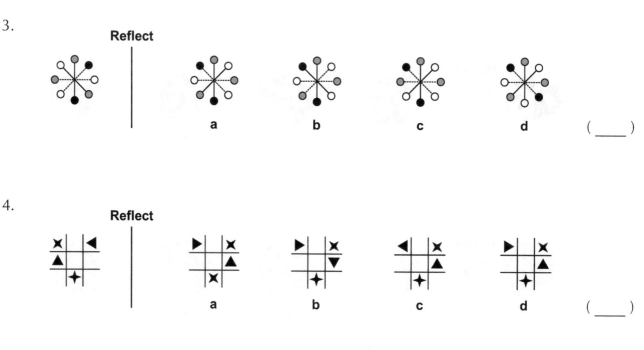

a     b     c     d     ( ___ )

4.

**Reflect**

a     b     c     d     ( ___ )

Rotation and Reflection

5.

**Reflect**

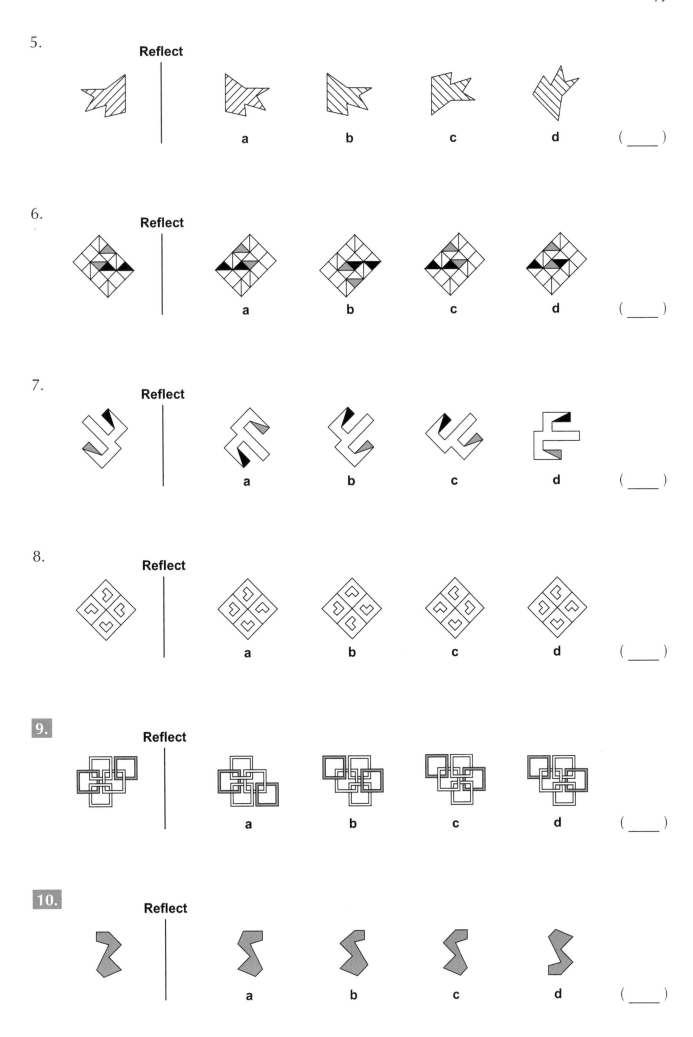

a        b        c        d    ( _____ )

6.

**Reflect**

a        b        c        d    ( _____ )

7.

**Reflect**

a        b        c        d    ( _____ )

8.

**Reflect**

a        b        c        d    ( _____ )

9.

**Reflect**

a        b        c        d    ( _____ )

10.

**Reflect**

a        b        c        d    ( _____ )

Rotation and Reflection

# Spatial Reasoning

# 3D Rotation

Work out which 3D figure in the grey box has been rotated to make the new 3D figure.
Example:

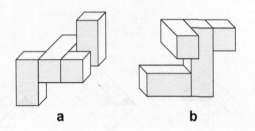

a

b

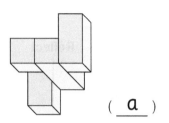

( _a_ )

Shape A has been rotated 180 degrees in the plane of the page.

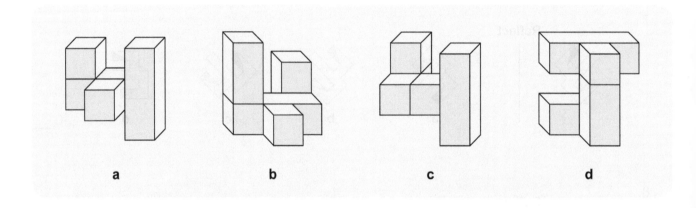

a          b          c          d

1.

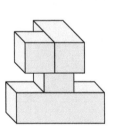

( ___ )

2.

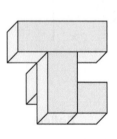

( ___ )

3.

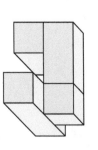

( ___ )

4.

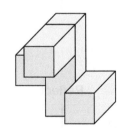

( ___ )

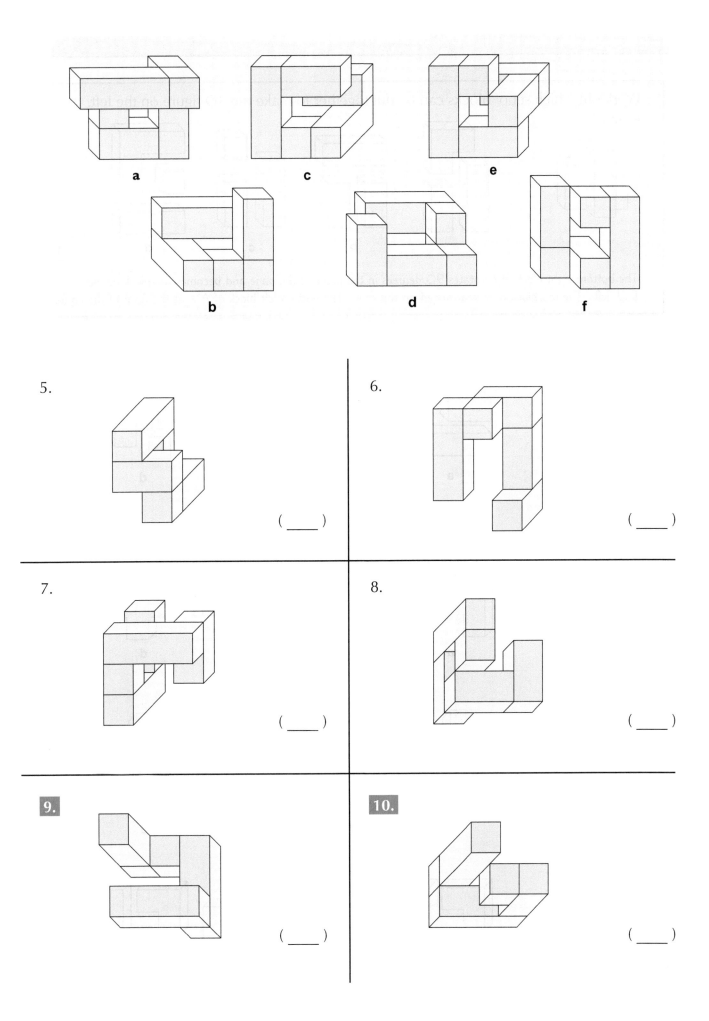

a

c

e

b

d

f

5.

( ___ )

6.

( ___ )

7.

( ___ )

8.

( ___ )

9.

( ___ )

10.

( ___ )

Spatial Reasoning

# 3D Building Blocks

Work out which set of blocks can be put together to make the 3D figure on the left.
Example:

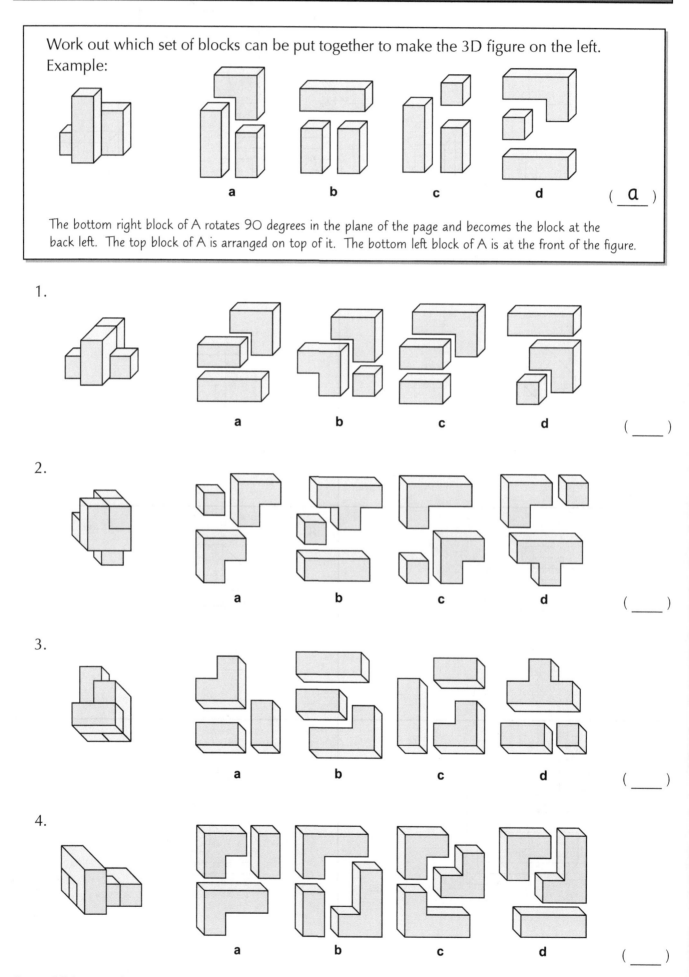

a          b          c          d          ( _a_ )

The bottom right block of A rotates 90 degrees in the plane of the page and becomes the block at the back left. The top block of A is arranged on top of it. The bottom left block of A is at the front of the figure.

1.

a          b          c          d          ( ___ )

2.

a          b          c          d          ( ___ )

3.

a          b          c          d          ( ___ )

4.

a          b          c          d          ( ___ )

5. ( ___ )

6. ( ___ )

7. ( ___ )

8. ( ___ )

**9.** ( ___ )

Spatial Reasoning

# 2D Views of 3D Shapes

Work out which option is a top-down 2D view of the 3D figure on the left.

Example:

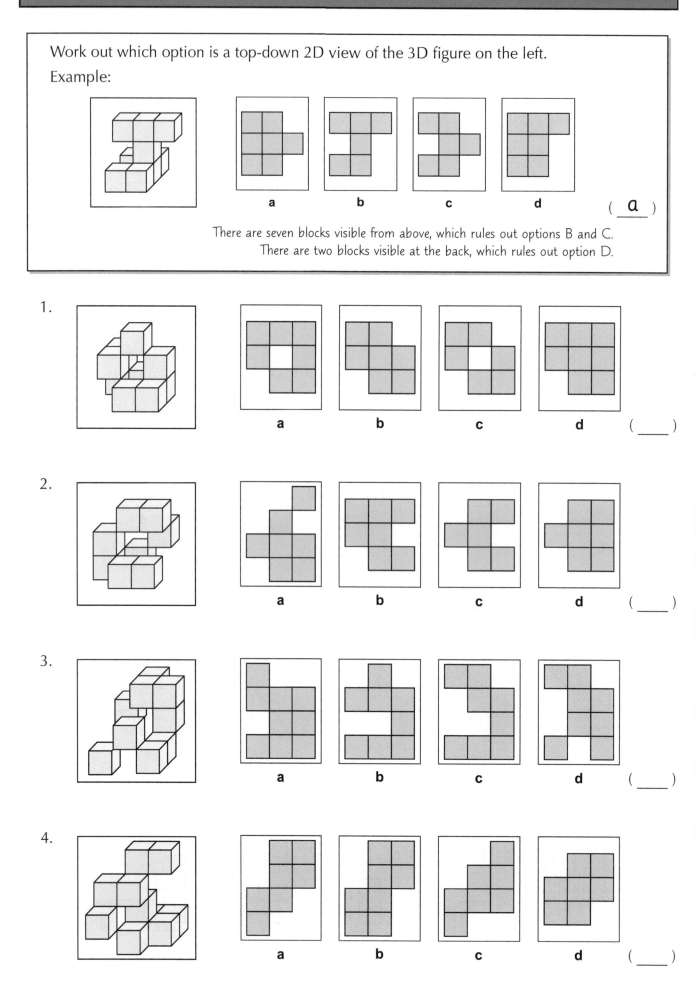

( _a_ )

There are seven blocks visible from above, which rules out options B and C.
There are two blocks visible at the back, which rules out option D.

1.                                                      a        b        c        d        ( ___ )

2.                                                      a        b        c        d        ( ___ )

3.                                                      a        b        c        d        ( ___ )

4.                                                      a        b        c        d        ( ___ )

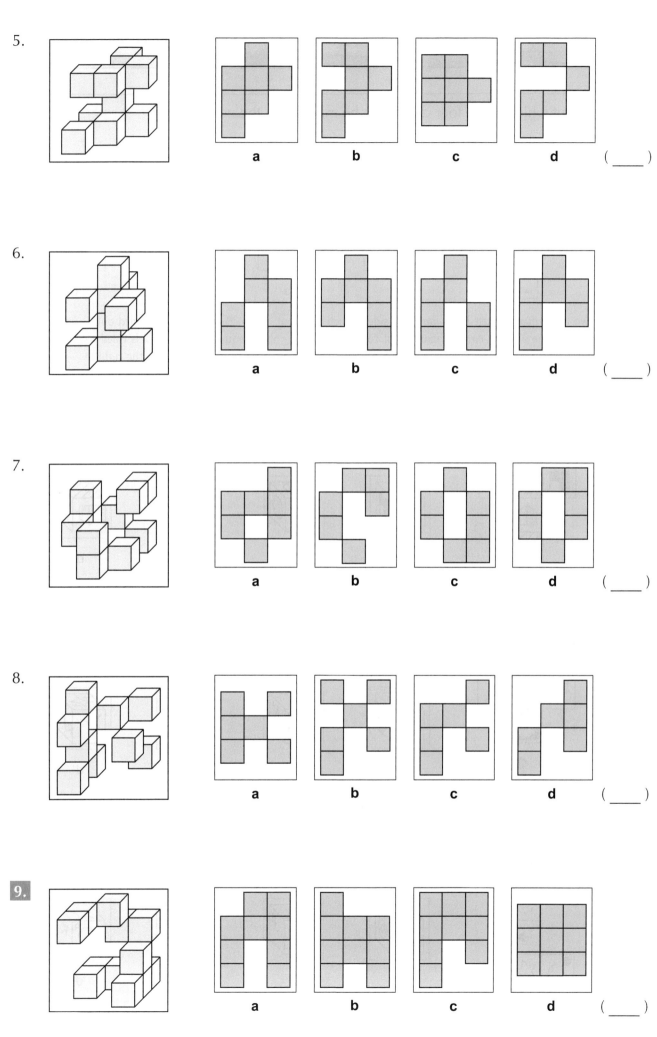

5. a b c d ( ____ )

6. a b c d ( ____ )

7. a b c d ( ____ )

8. a b c d ( ____ )

9. a b c d ( ____ )

# Cubes and Nets

Work out which of the four cubes can be made from the net.

Example:

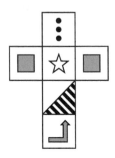

a         b         c         d

The two grey squares must be on opposite sides, which rules out option A. Option B is ruled out because the line of black circles should point towards the star, not the square. Option D is ruled out because if the black and white triangle was on the front and the grey square was on the right, the face on the top would be the white star.

( **C** )

1.

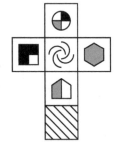

a         b         c         d    (     )

2.

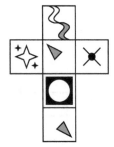

a         b         c         d    (     )

3.

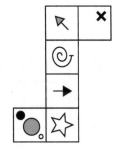

a         b         c         d    (     )

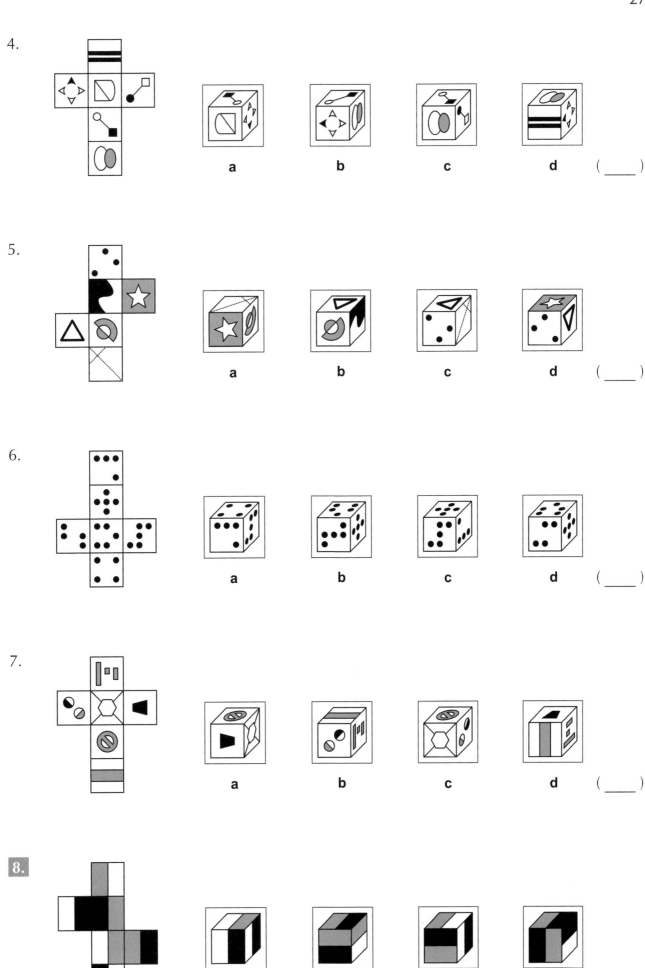

4.

    a           b           c           d   ( _____ )

5.

    a           b           c           d   ( _____ )

6.

    a           b           c           d   ( _____ )

7.

    a           b           c           d   ( _____ )

**8.**

    a           b           c           d   ( _____ )

# Fold Along the Line

Work out which option shows the figure on the left when folded along the dotted line.
Example:

        **a**       **b**       **c**       **d**  ( _C_ )

Options A and B are ruled out because the part of the figure that has been folded is the wrong shape. Option D is ruled out because the fold line has moved.

1.

    **a**    **b**    **c**    **d**  ( ___ )

2.

    **a**    **b**    **c**    **d**  ( ___ )

3.

    **a**    **b**    **c**    **d**  ( ___ )

4.

    **a**    **b**    **c**    **d**  ( ___ )

5.

    **a**    **b**    **c**    **d**  ( ___ )

29

**6.**

a     b     c     d     ( ___ )

**7.**

a     b     c     d     ( ___ )

**8.**

a     b     c     d     ( ___ )

**9.**

a     b     c     d     ( ___ )

**10.**

a     b     c     d     ( ___ )

**11.**

a     b     c     d     ( ___ )

Spatial Reasoning

# Fold and Punch

A square is folded and then a hole is punched, as shown on the left.
Work out which option shows the square when unfolded.

Example:

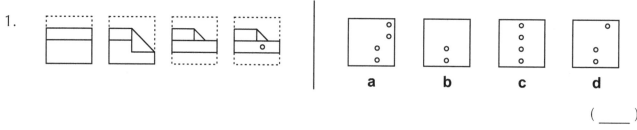

( __d__ )

Unfold the figure, one fold at a time:

1.

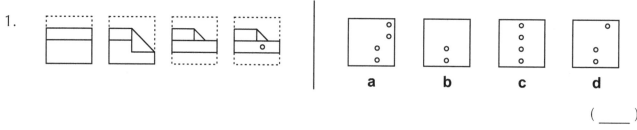

a     b     c     d

( ___ )

2.

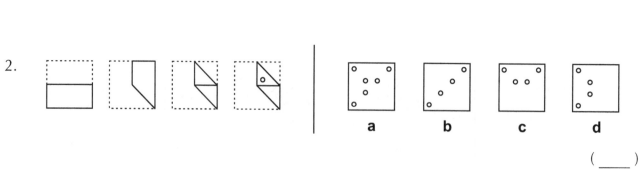

a     b     c     d

( ___ )

3.

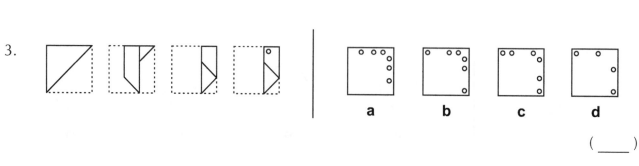

a     b     c     d

( ___ )

4.

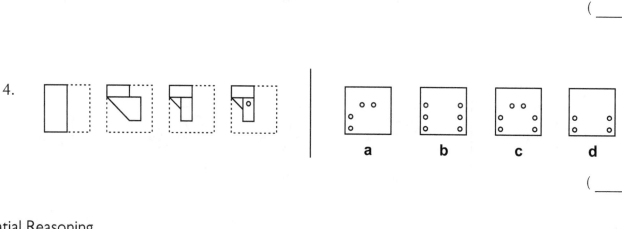

a     b     c     d

( ___ )

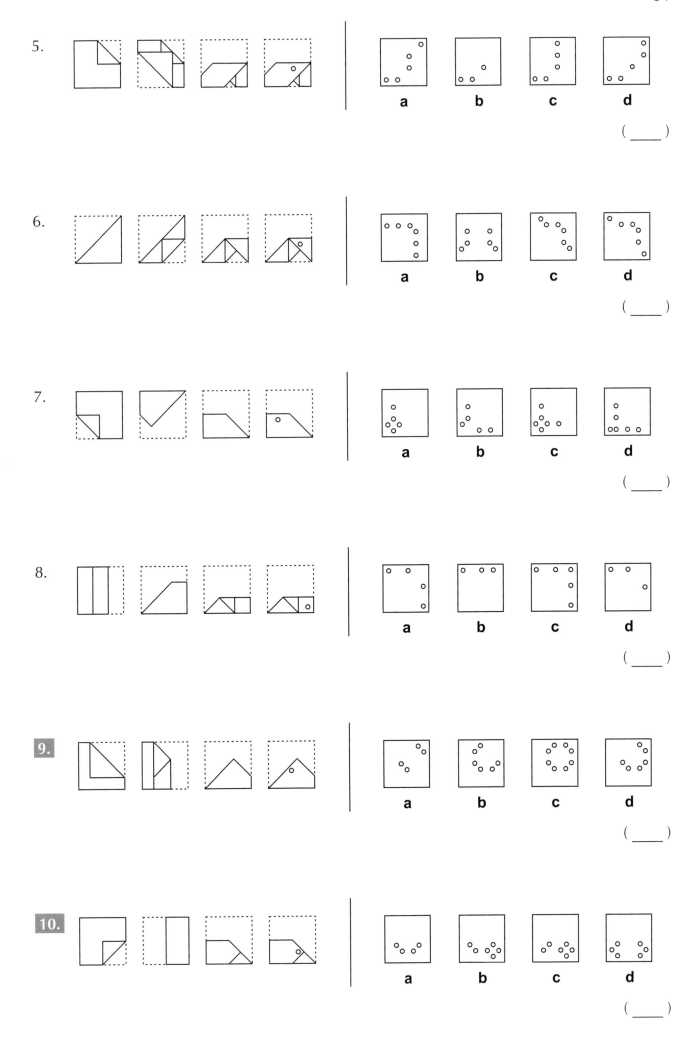

31

5.

( _____ )

6.

( _____ )

7.

( _____ )

8.

( _____ )

9.

( _____ )

10.

( _____ )

Spatial Reasoning

# Assessment Test 1

This book contains three assessment tests to help you improve your NVR skills.

Allow 45 minutes to do each test and work as quickly and as carefully as you can.

If you want to attempt each test more than once, you will need to print **multiple-choice answer sheets** for these questions from our website — go to cgpbooks.co.uk/11plus/answer-sheets or scan the QR code on the right. If you'd prefer to answer them in standard write-in format, just circle the letter underneath your answer.

Answer Sheets

## Find the Figure Like the First Two

For each of the questions below there are two figures that are like each other in some way. Find which of the four figures on the right is most like the two figures on the left.

**Example:**

  |

          a            b           c           d

**Answer: c**

---

**1**

  |

          a            b           c           d

---

**2**

  |

          a            b           c           d

---

**3**

  |

          a            b           c           d

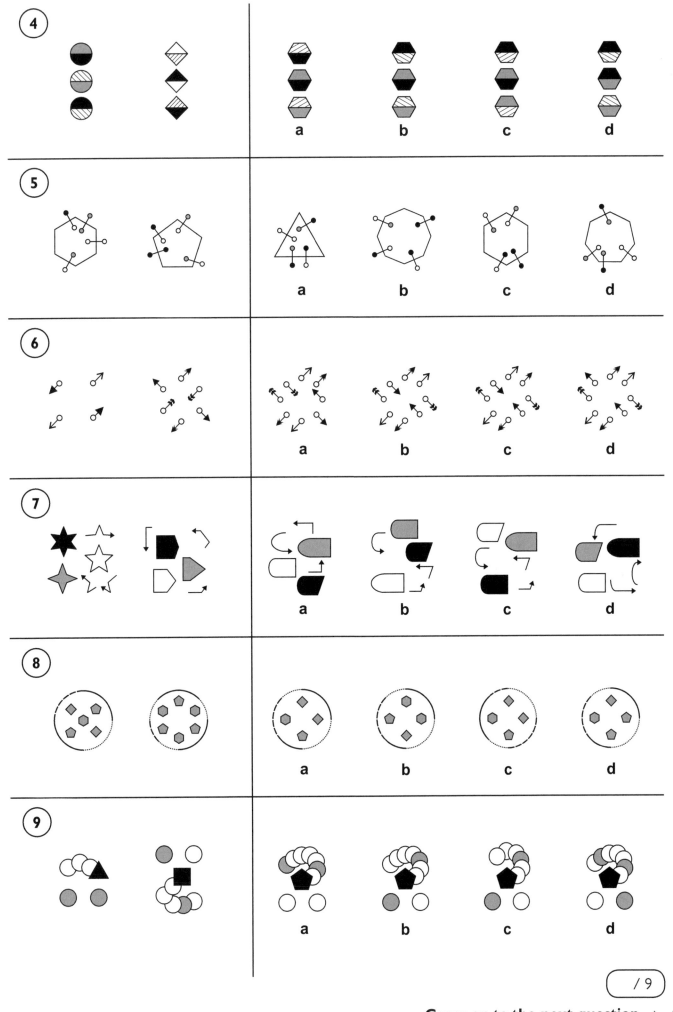

**Carry on to the next question → →**

Assessment Test 1

# Section 2 — Rotate the Figure

Work out which option would look like the figure on the left if it was rotated.

**Example:**

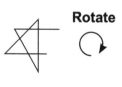 Rotate

a

b

c

d

**Answer: b**

**1**

 Rotate

a

b

c

d

**2**

 Rotate

a

b

c

d

**3**

Rotate

a

b

c

d

**4**

Rotate

a

b

c

d

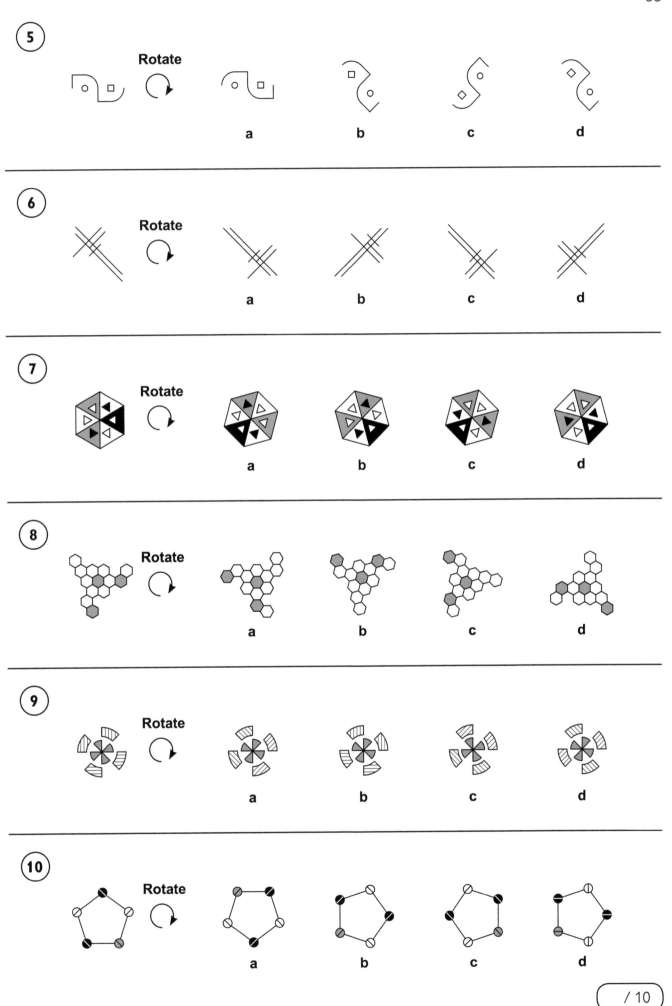

**Carry on to the next question → →**

Assessment Test 1

# Section 3 — Complete the Pair

Look at how the first two figures are changed, and then work out which option would look like the third figure if you changed it in the same way.

**Example:**

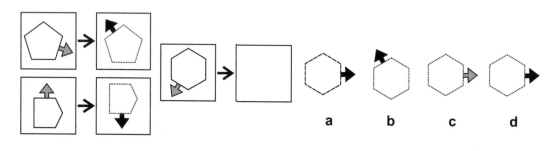

**Answer: d**

**1**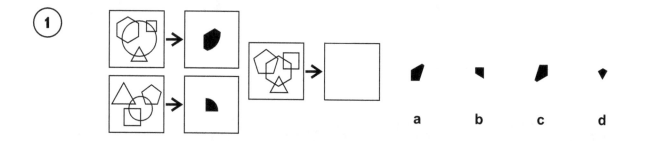

**2**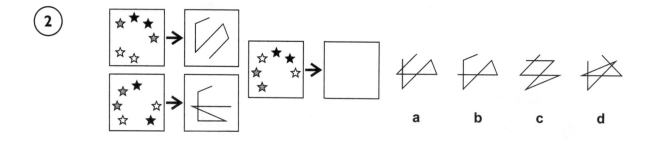

**3**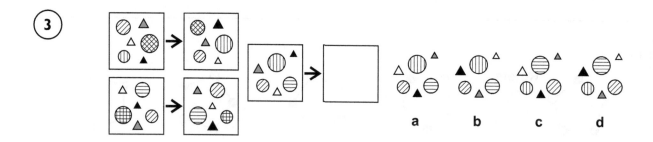

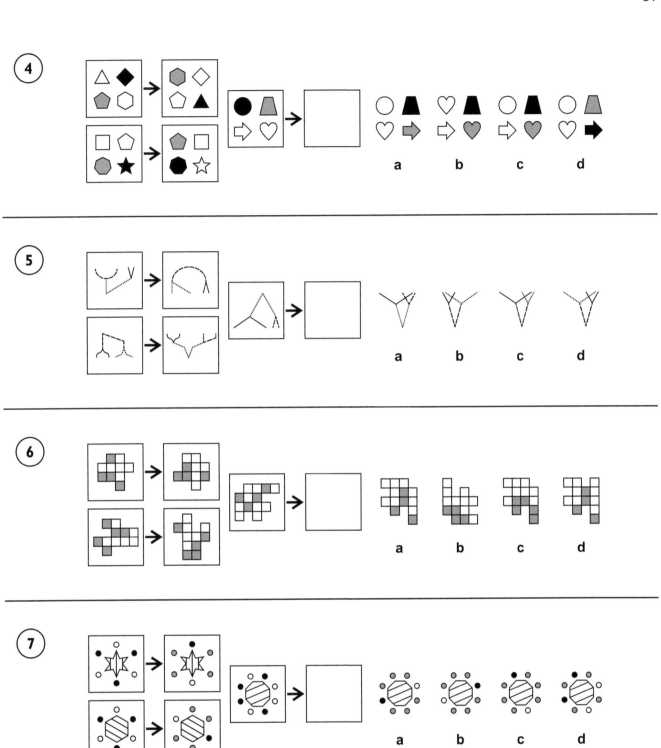

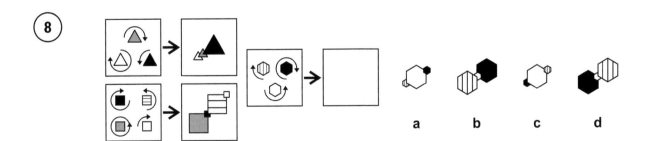

# Section 4 — Cubes and Nets

Work out which of the four cubes can be made from the net.

**Example:**

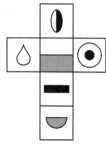

a

b

c

d

**Answer: c**

**1**

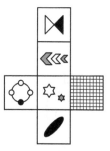

a

b

c

d

**2**

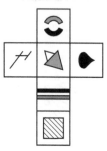

a

b

c

d

**3**

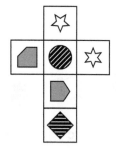

a

b

c

d

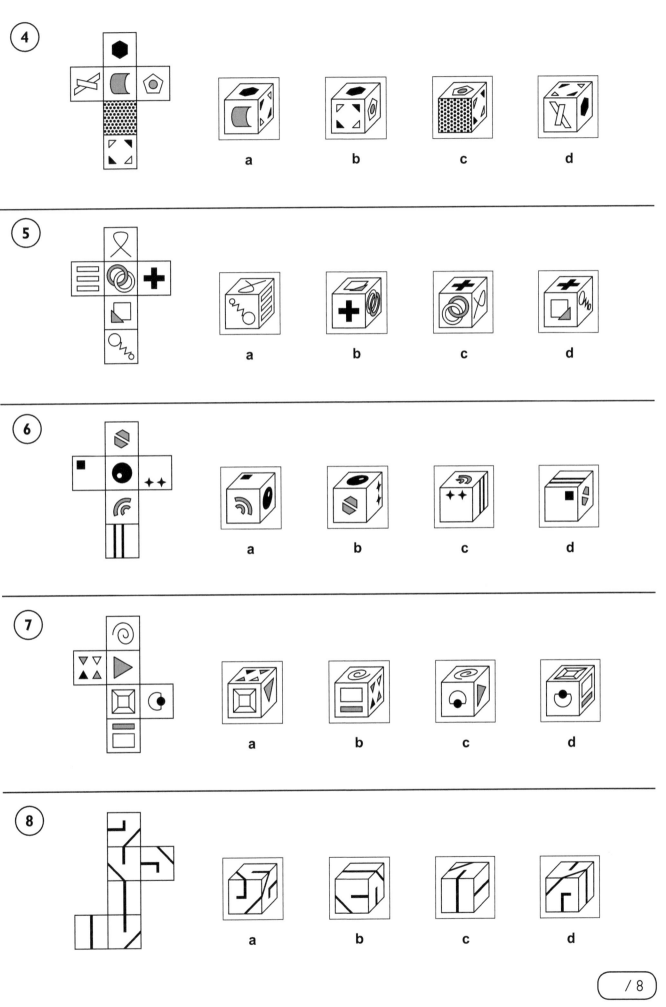

# Section 5 — Fold and Punch

A square is folded and then a hole is punched, as shown on the left.
Work out which option shows the square when unfolded.

**Example:**

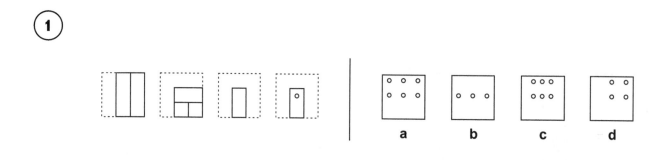

a     b     c     d

**Answer: d**

**1**

a     b     c     d

**2**

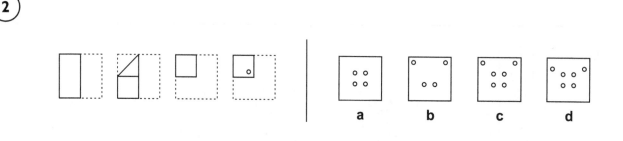

a     b     c     d

**3**

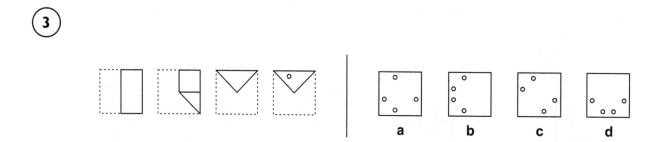

a     b     c     d

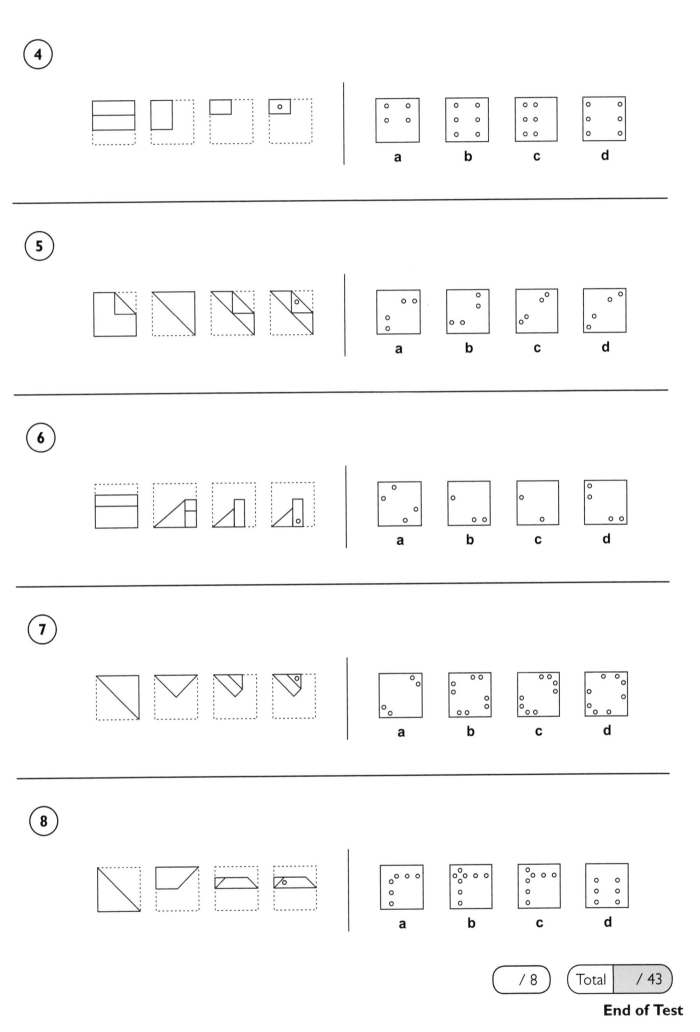

# Assessment Test 2

Allow 45 minutes to do this test and work as quickly and as carefully as you can.

You can print **multiple-choice answer sheets** for these questions from our website —
go to cgpbooks.co.uk/11plus/answer-sheets or scan the QR code on the right. If you'd prefer
to answer them in standard write-in format, just circle the letter underneath your answer.

**Answer Sheets**

---

## Section 1 — Complete the Square Grid

Work out which of the options best fits in place of the missing square in the grid.

**Example:**

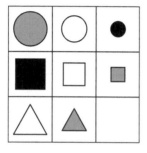   

a        b        c        d

**Answer: d**

---

**1**

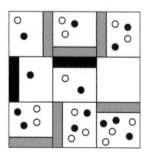 

a        b        c        d

---

**2**

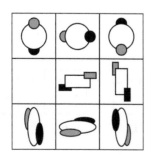   

a        b        c        d

---

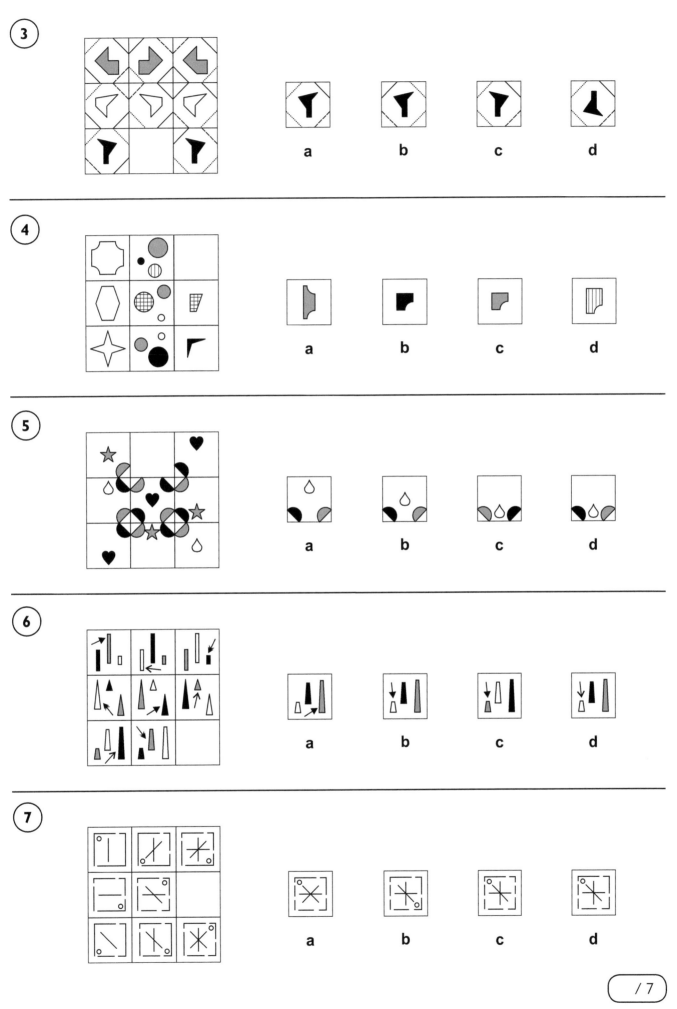

# Section 2 — Odd One Out

Find the figure in each row that is most unlike the other figures.

**Example:**

a       b       c       d       e

**Answer: a**

**1**

a       b       c       d       e

**2**

a       b       c       d       e

**3**

a       b       c       d       e

**4**

a       b       c       d       e

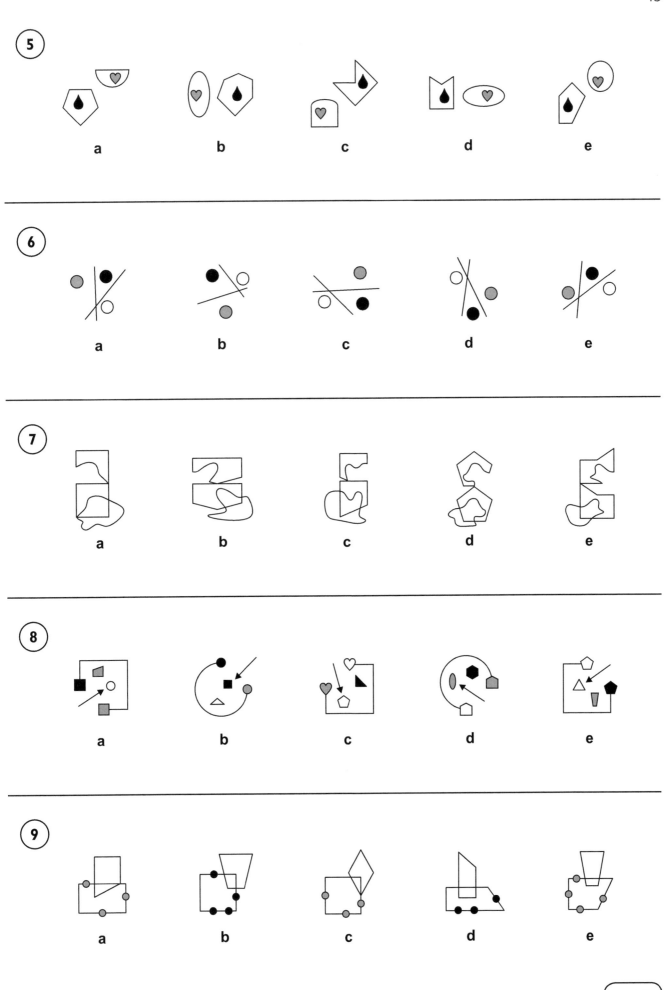

# Section 3 — Complete the Series

Work out which of the options best fits in place of the missing square in the series.

**Example:**

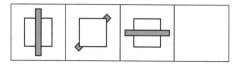

a      b      c      d

**Answer: d**

**1**

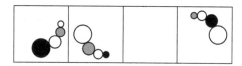

a      b      c      d

**2**

a      b      c      d

**3**

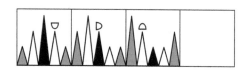

a      b      c      d

**4**

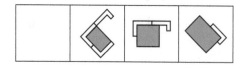

a      b      c      d

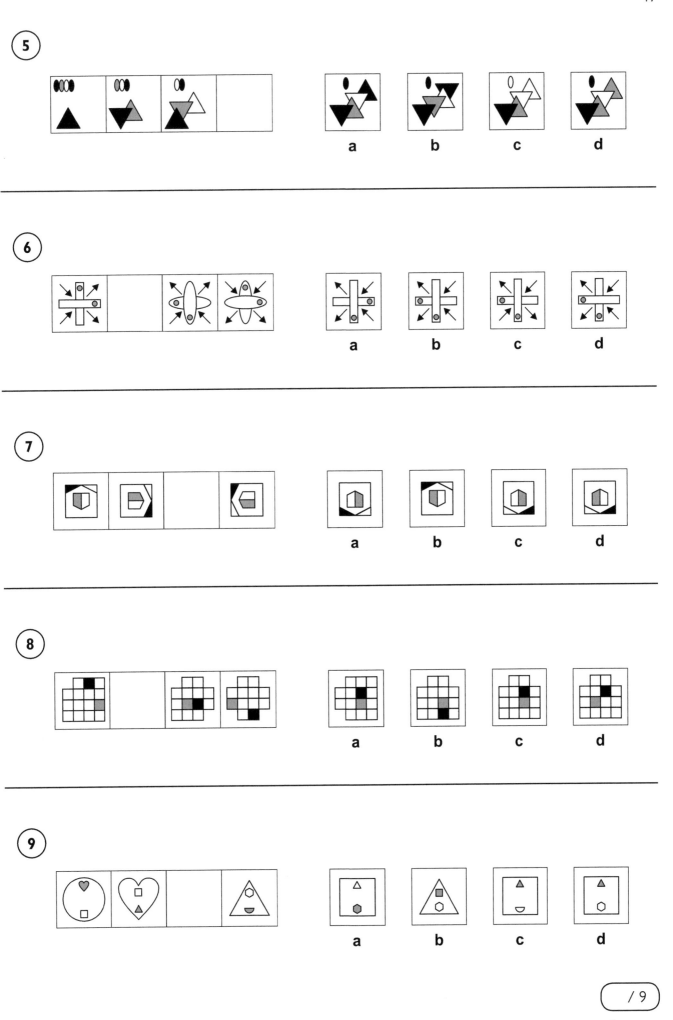

**Carry on to the next question → →**

Assessment Test 2

# Section 4 — 3D Rotation

Work out which 3D figure in the grey box has been rotated to make the new 3D figure.

**Example:**

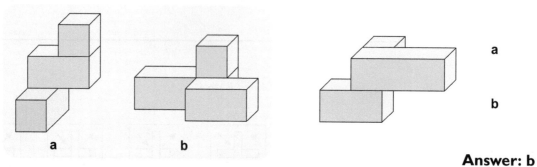

a

b

**Answer: b**

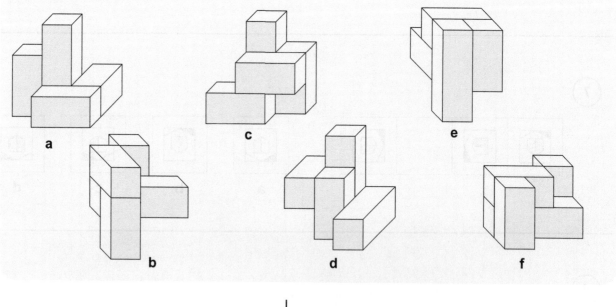

a    b    c    d    e    f

(1)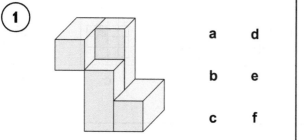

a    d

b    e

c    f

(2)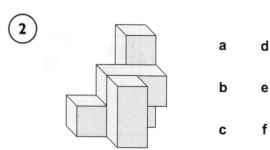

a    d

b    e

c    f

(3)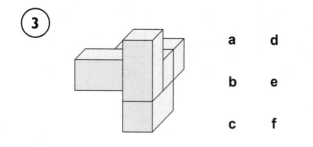

a    d

b    e

c    f

(4)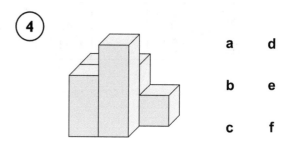

a    d

b    e

c    f

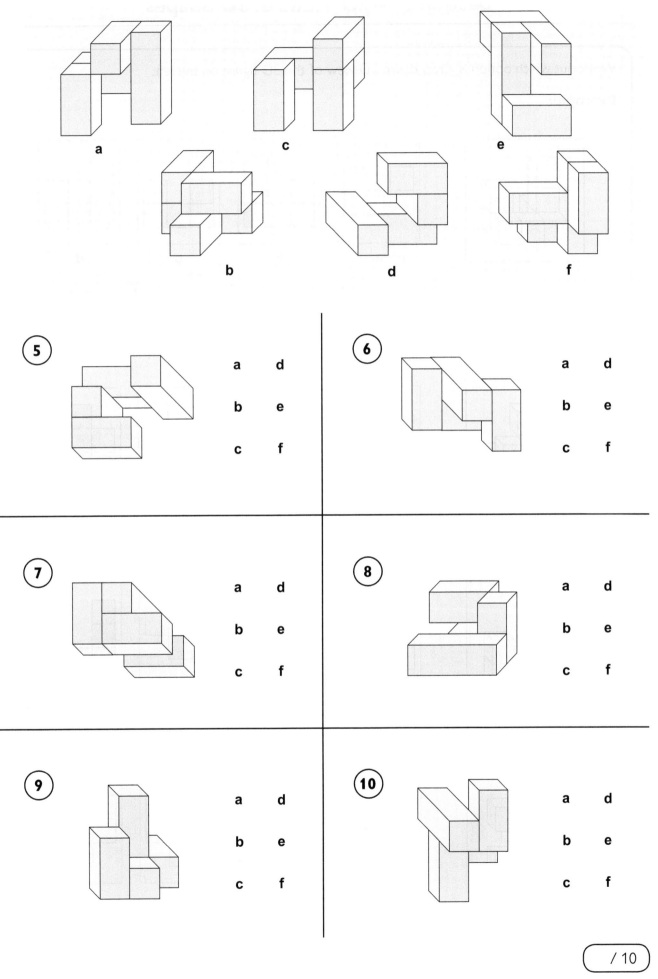

a

c

e

b

d

f

⑤

a d

b e

c f

⑥

a d

b e

c f

⑦

a d

b e

c f

⑧

a d

b e

c f

⑨

a d

b e

c f

⑩

a d

b e

c f

/ 10

**Carry on to the next question** → →

Assessment Test 2

# Section 5 — 2D Views of 3D Shapes

Work out which option is a top-down 2D view of the 3D figure on the left.

**Example:**

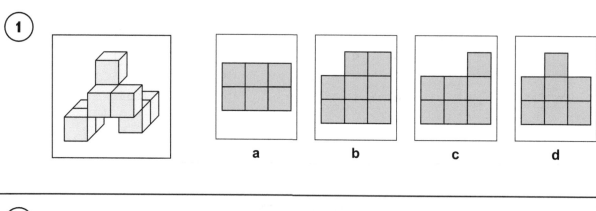

Answer: c

**1**

**2**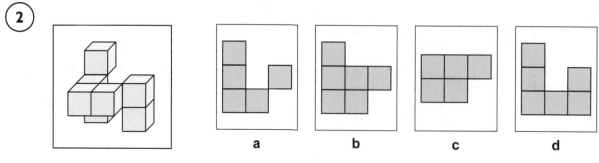

**3**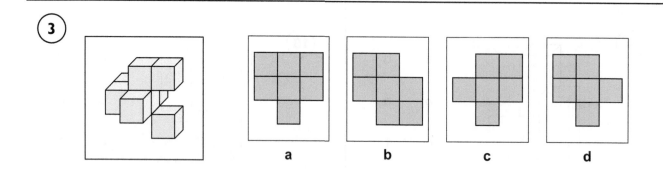

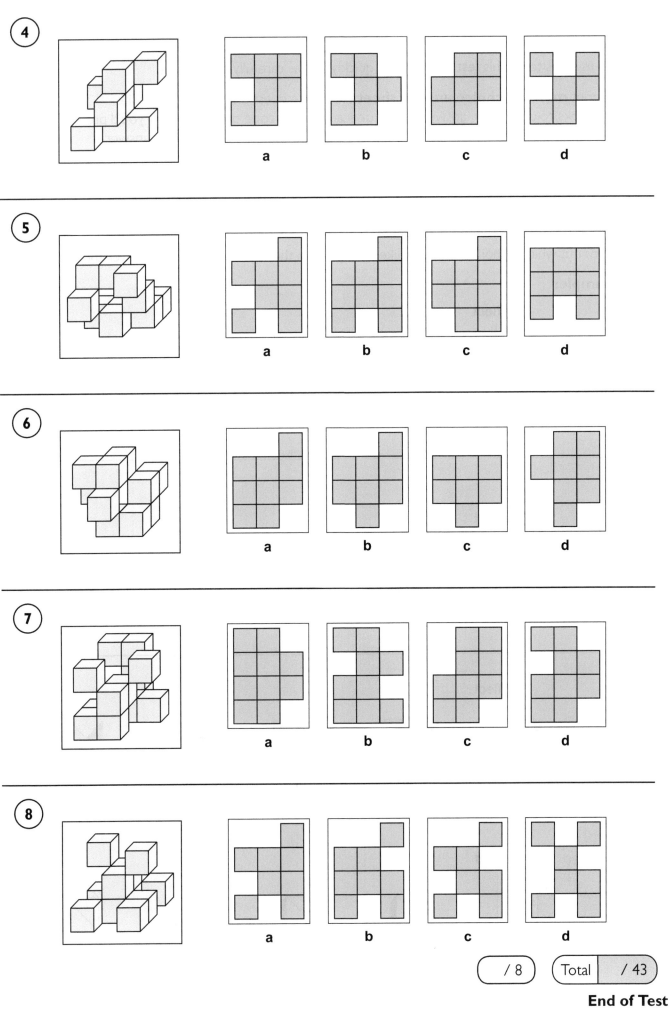

# Assessment Test 3

Allow 45 minutes to do this test and work as quickly and as carefully as you can.

You can print **multiple-choice answer sheets** for these questions from our website — go to cgpbooks.co.uk/11plus/answer-sheets or scan the QR code on the right. If you'd prefer to answer them in standard write-in format, just circle the letter underneath your answer.

**Answer Sheets**

## Section 1 — Reflect the Figure

Work out which option would look like the figure on the left if it was reflected over the line.

**Example:**

**Reflect**

a

b

c

d

**Answer: a**

**1**

**Reflect**

a          b          c          d

**2**

**Reflect**

a          b          c          d

**3**

**Reflect**

a          b          c          d

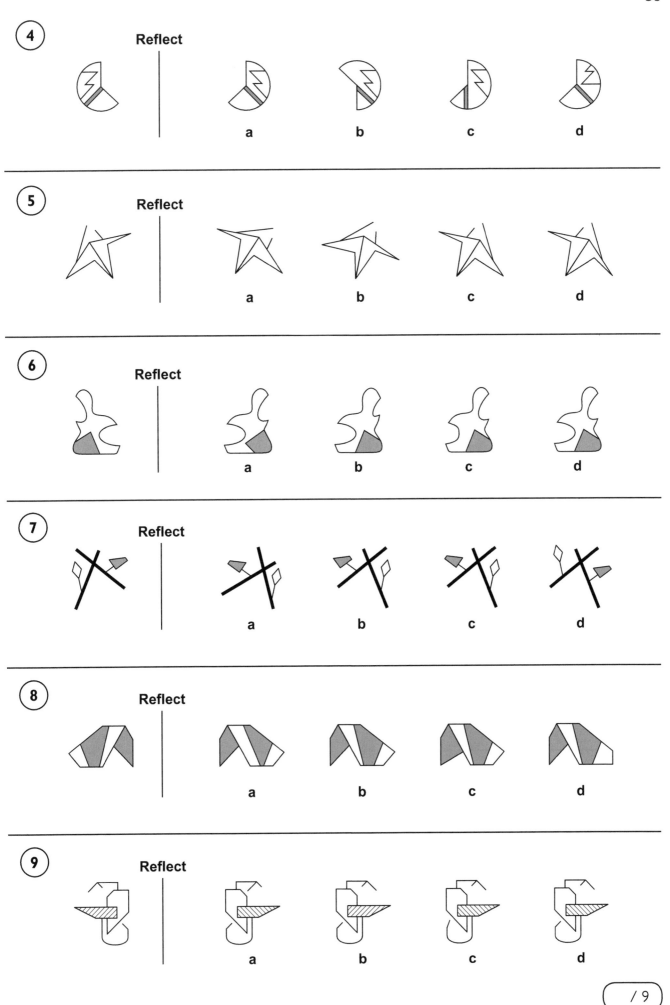

# Section 2 — Fold Along the Line

Work out which option shows the figure on the left when folded along the dotted line.

**Example:**

a        b        c        d

**Answer: a**

**1**

a        b        c        d

**2**

a        b        c        d

**3**

a        b        c        d

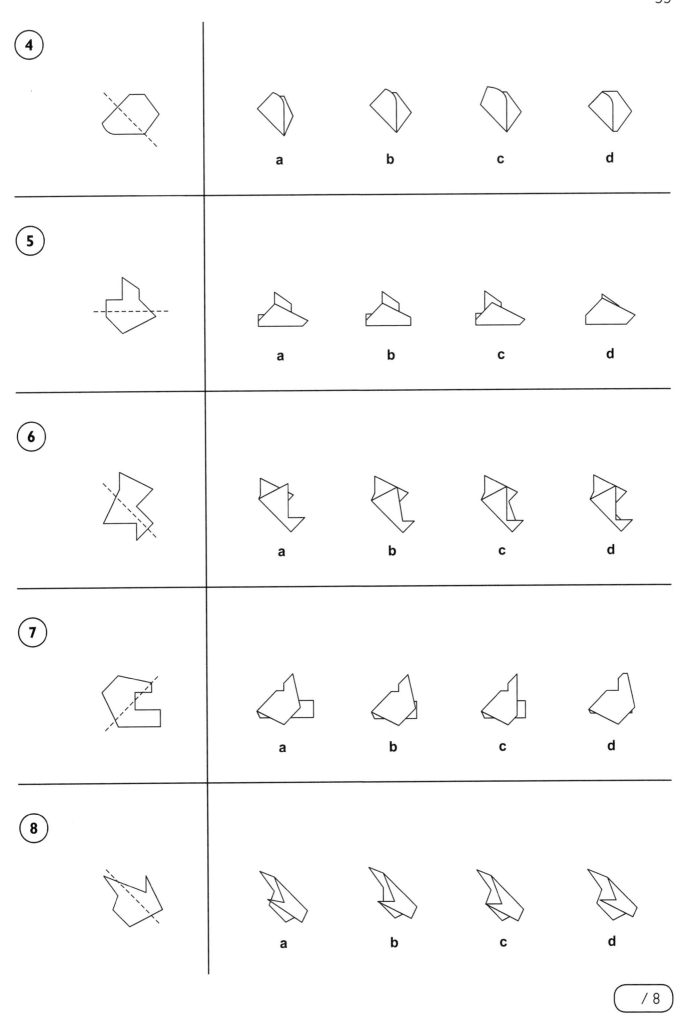

# Section 3 — Complete the Hexagonal Grid

Work out which of the options best fits in place of the missing hexagon in the grid.

**Example:**

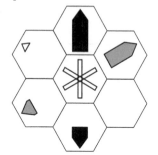     

                                      a             b             c             d

**Answer: b**

**(1)**

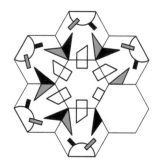     

                                      a             b             c             d

**(2)**

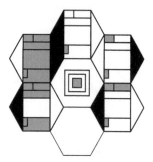     

                                      a             b             c             d

**(3)**

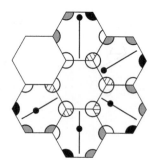     

                                      a             b             c             d

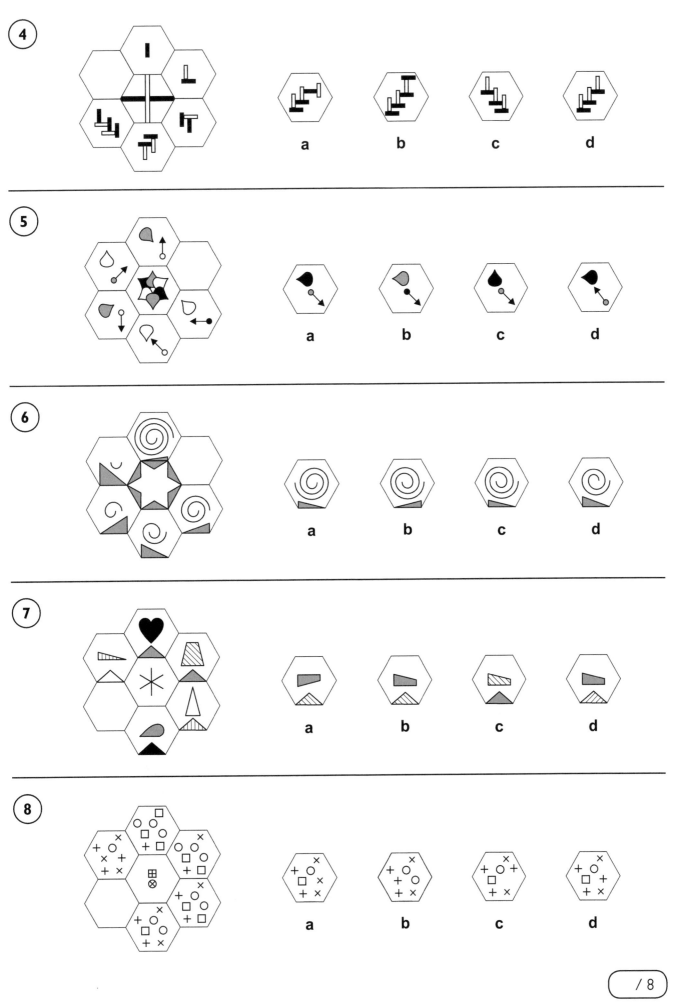

# Section 4 — Changing Bugs

Look at how the first bug changes to become the second bug.
Then work out which option would look like the third bug if you changed it in the same way.

**Example:**

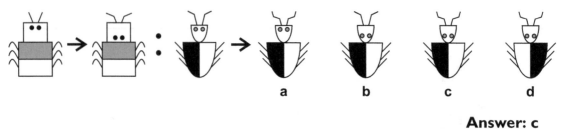

**Answer: c**

**1**

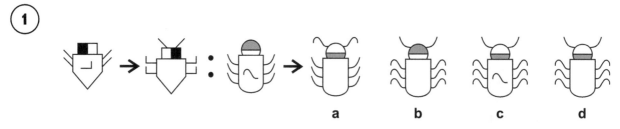

**2**

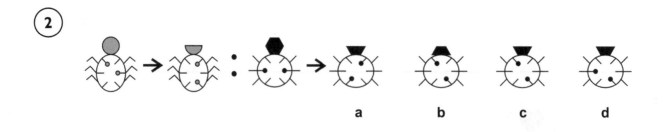

**3**

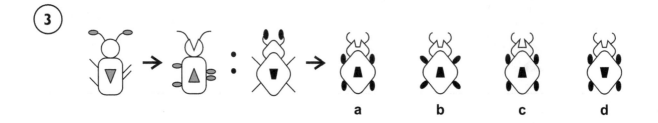

**4**

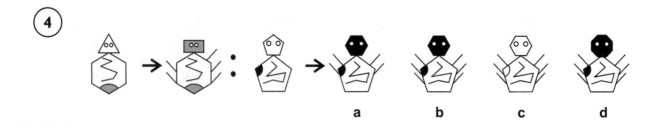

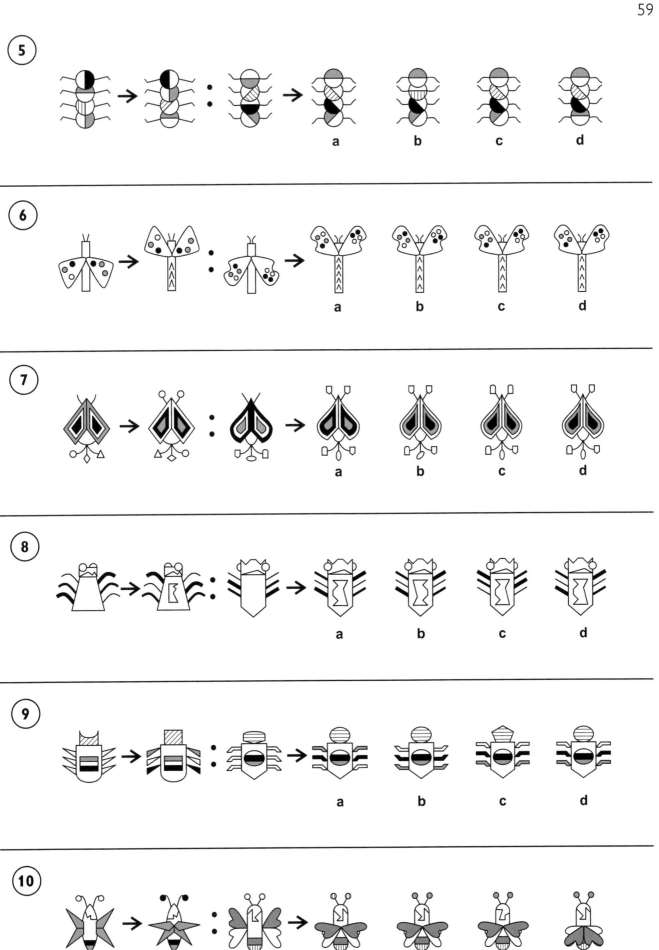

# Section 5 — 3D Building Blocks

Work out which set of blocks can be put together to make the 3D figure on the left.

**Example:**

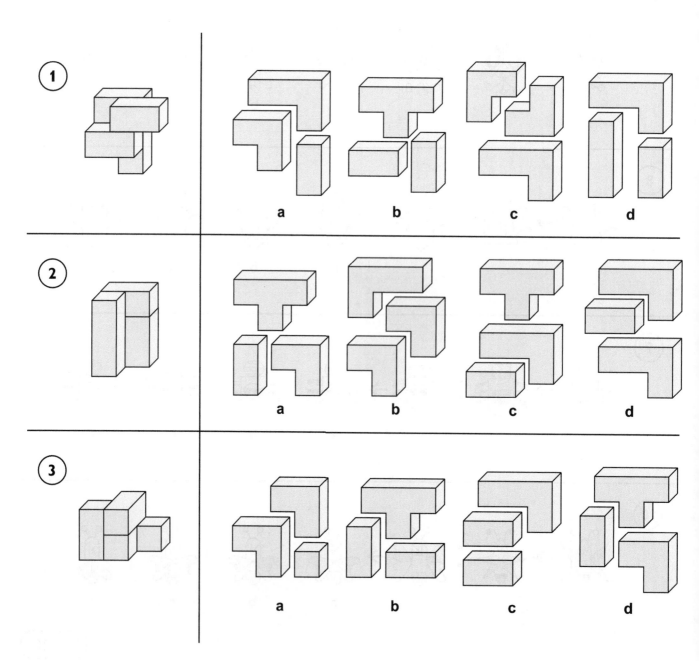

Answer: b

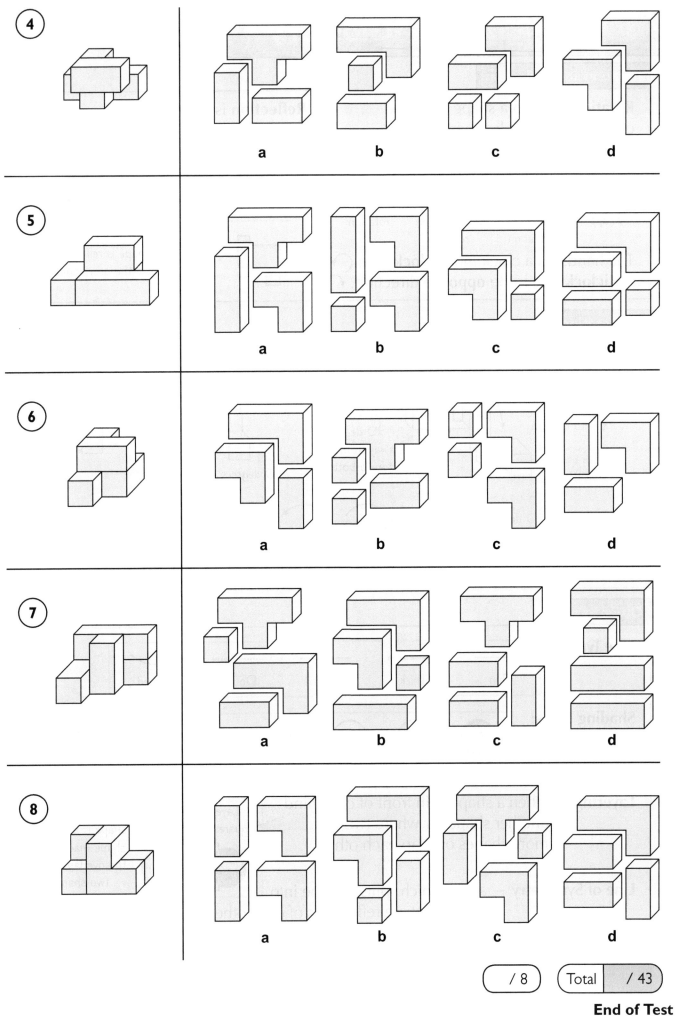

# Glossary

## Rotation and Reflection

**Rotation** is when a shape is **turned** clockwise or anticlockwise.

Example shape    90 degrees clockwise rotation    45 degrees anticlockwise rotation    180 degrees rotation

The hands on a clock move **clockwise**:
**Anticlockwise** is the **opposite** direction:

**Reflection** is when something is **mirrored** over a visible or invisible line.

The black shape is reflected across to make the white shape.

The black shape is reflected down to make the grey shape.

## 3D Rotation

There are **three planes** that a 3D shape can be rotated in.

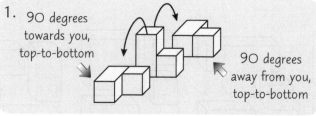

1. 90 degrees towards you, top-to-bottom
90 degrees away from you, top-to-bottom

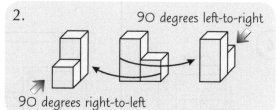

2. 90 degrees left-to-right
90 degrees right-to-left

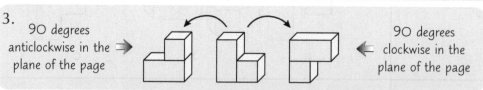

3. 90 degrees anticlockwise in the plane of the page
90 degrees clockwise in the plane of the page

## Other terms

**Line Types:**

Thin    Thick    Dashed    Dotted    Curved

**Shading Types:**

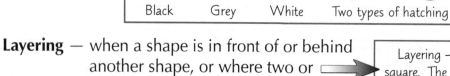

Black    Grey    White    Two types of hatching    Cross-hatched    Spotted

**Layering** — when a shape is in front of or behind another shape, or where two or more shapes overlap each other.

Layering — the circle is in front of the square. The right-hand shape is a cut-out shape made from the overlap of the two shapes.

**Line of Symmetry** — a line which splits a shape into halves that are reflections of each other.

 This triangle has three lines of symmetry.

 A square has four lines of symmetry.

 This shape has one line of symmetry.

# Answers

## Similarities and Differences

### Pages 2-3 — Odd One Out

**1) E**
In all other figures, the curved line goes from one corner of the large shape to the next corner of the large shape.

**2) A**
In all other figures, the small grey shapes have fewer sides than the larger white shape that they are inside.

**3) D**
In all other figures, the number of grey circles is equal to the number of columns of circles.

**4) C**
In all other figures, the arrow with the solid arrowhead is pointing at the smallest angle in the shape.

**5) E**
In all other figures, the number of white sections in the circle is equal to the number of white raindrops.

**6) E**
In all other figures, the white shape has been rotated 45 degrees clockwise to give the grey shape.

**7) B**
In all other figures, the small hatched shape is the shape made by the overlap of the clear and grey shapes reflected across.

**8) C**
In all other figures, each grey dot comes after the point on the star it is closest to, moving in a clockwise direction around the star. Each black dot comes before the point on the star it is closest to, moving in a clockwise direction around the star.

**9) D**
In all other figures, the number of sides of the hatched, overlapped part of the figure is the same as the number of sides of the shape with the most sides.

**10) A**
In all other figures, the direction of the arrow matches the direction of the hatching in the shape that has at least one line of symmetry.

### Pages 4-5 — Find the Figure Like the First Two or Three

**1) B**
All figures must have two grey circles, one black circle and one white circle.

**2) B**
All figures must be a rotation of the same shape.

**3) C**
All figures must have a large shape that has exactly half shaded grey. The small shapes should be smaller copies of the large shape, excluding shading.

**4) D**
All figures must have two copies of one of the shapes, one smaller than the other. The arrow points to the smaller copy.

**5) D**
All figures must have a shape that has an arrow pointing from one of its corners. The number of arrowheads on this arrow must be one less than the number of sides of the shape.

**6) B**
All figures must have a star at the front, and the shape at the back of the figure must be shaded black.

**7) C**
All figures must contain a raindrop in a four-sided shape, and a 45 degree anticlockwise rotation of the raindrop in a five-sided shape.

**8) A**
All figures must have one more grey circle than the number of rectangles.

**9) B**
All figures must contain two fewer black shapes at the front than the number of sides on the large white shape. The hatching in the smaller white shape must be diagonal.

## Pairs, Series and Grids

### Pages 6-7 — Complete the Pair

**1) B**
The ends of the dashed lines are connected to form a new shape. The hatching of the shape is in the direction of any solid lines.

**2) B**
The lines are moved so the dots on the lines overlap the dot in the grey shape. The grey shape is then cut into pieces along the lines, and the lines and dots are removed.

**3) D**
The largest shape moves to the back. The middle-sized shape moves to the front, is reflected downwards and swaps shadings with the smallest shape.

**4) D**
The grey and black shapes swap sizes. Then the white and grey shapes are combined into one white shape, and the black shape is cut out. The resulting shape is split into quarters.

**5) A**
The white shape is replaced by two new shapes in the adjacent corners of the square. Going clockwise, the shape has one more side. Going anticlockwise, the shape is half of the original shape. The top shape is shaded grey and the bottom shape is shaded black.

**6) A**
The outline of each shape changes to dotted where it overlaps both of the other two shapes, and to dashed where it overlaps neither of the other two shapes.

**7) C**
The two outer shapes swap places, then each pair of shapes swap shadings.

**8) C**
The lines are reflected across the centre of the figure and combined with the original lines to form a new shape. The circles are reflected across and change from being behind the line to being in front of the line, and vice versa.

**9) B**
The shape is divided in half along the direction of the arrow with the matching line style. Only the half nearest the arrow is kept. The line style is then changed to match the two-headed arrow.

**10) C**
Each black circle moves to the next line on its right, and back to the left-most line when it reaches the right-most line. Each white circle moves to the next line on its left, and back to the right-most line when it reaches the left-most line.

## Pages 8-9 — Complete the Series

**1) B**

In each series square, the star gets smaller and the hexagon gets larger. The shapes alternate between black and white shading.

**2) A**

The squares in this series are in two pairs. In each pair, the figure is reflected across, the shadings swap between black and white, and the figure extends on the right-hand side.

**3) A**

In each series square, the circle moves up and alternates between the right side and the left side. The other shape gains an extra side and moves across the series square, alternating between the bottom and the top.

**4) C**

In each series square, the top grey circle moves right and the bottom grey circle moves left. The white cross and circle rotate together 45 degrees anticlockwise. The lines that are attached to the grey circles alternate between being behind and in front of the cross.

**5) D**

In each series square, the shadings of the circles move one place to the left. Both arrows move clockwise around the corners of the series square, and each arrow points towards the circle with the same colour shading.

**6) B**

In each series square, one more star segment turns grey, moving one place clockwise around the star. The black shading moves two steps anticlockwise around the star, covering any grey shading it would overlap with.

**7) A**

The squares in this series are in two pairs. In each pair, the dotted line divides the shapes into groups: in the left-hand square the shapes in each group have matching shading, and in the right-hand square the shapes in each group have the same number of sides.

**8) C**

In each series square, the hatching of the rectangle matches the hatching of the bottom circle in the previous series square. The hatching of the top circle matches the hatching of the rectangle in the previous series square.

**9) D**

In each series square, the figure rotates 90 degrees clockwise about the centre of the square, then the heart shape rotates 90 degrees about its own centre.

**10) A**

In each series square, the grey rectangle containing the triangle rotates 45 degrees anticlockwise and the grey rectangle containing the L-shape rotates 90 degrees anticlockwise. The overlap of the two rectangles is shaded white.

**11) A**

In each series square, the circle in the top-left connects to the next circle, working left to right across the series square. The circle in the bottom-right connects to the next circle, but working bottom to top up the series square.

**12) C**

In each series square, the shape moves to the next space between the lines, moving in a clockwise direction. The shape changes to a smaller copy of the shape created by the lines in the previous space. Each line type moves one place to the next line, moving in a clockwise direction around the lines.

## Pages 10-11 — Complete the Square Grid

**1) B**

The direction of the diagonal line is the same in each grid square in a row. The half of the grid square and inner shape that is shaded black alternates within each row. Each shape appears once in each row and column.

**2) C**

In each row, there is one grid square with two overlapping shapes. The other two grid squares in the row contain shapes created by cutting one overlapping shape out of the other.

**3) A**

Working from left to right, the shape rotates 90 degrees clockwise in each grid square and the X moves one place clockwise around the corners of the shape.

**4) D**

Working from left to right, each grid square loses a dashed horizontal line and gains a solid vertical line. Dashed lines should not move positions.

**5) C**

Working from left to right, the number of black hearts in each grid square decreases by one and the number of white hearts is halved.

**6) A**

There is one of each type of spiral (2 turns, 3 turns and 4 turns) in each row and column. Working from left to right, the direction of the spiral (working from the centre outwards) alternates between clockwise and anticlockwise and the end of the spiral rotates 90 degrees clockwise.

**7) D**

Working from left to right, the number of times the dotted line and the solid line overlap increases by one in each grid square. In each row, the black circle appears in three different places: on the end of the dotted line, on the end of the solid line and on the end of neither line.

**8) C**

Working from left to right, the arrow rotates 90 degrees clockwise in each grid square. The hatching rotates 45 degrees anticlockwise. Each corner shape in the left-hand grid square reflects across into the middle grid square and then reflects across again to the other side of the middle grid square. It reflects across once more into the right-hand grid square.

**9) B**

Working from top to bottom, an extra segment of the circle is shaded grey. The star alternates between being in a white segment and a grey segment of the circle.

**10) C**

Working from left to right, the number of right angles increases by one in each grid square. Each type of shading appears once in each row and column.

## Pages 12-13 — Complete the Hexagonal Grid

**1) C**

Going in a clockwise direction from the top hexagon, the figure gains a semicircle. Each hexagon alternates between having left-hand semicircles and right-hand semicircles and between having a black centre semicircle and a white centre semicircle.

**2) B**

Going in a clockwise direction from the top hexagon, the arrow rotates 60 degrees clockwise. An extra dot is added to the outline of the arrow, moving in a clockwise direction around the arrow.

**3) D**

The circles reflect across the middle of the hexagonal grid.

**4) C**

Going in a clockwise direction, each outer hexagon rotates 60 degrees.

**5) A**

Going in an anticlockwise direction from the top hexagon, one new circle and cross are added each time. The added circle alternates between black and white.

**6) A**

Going in a clockwise direction from the top hexagon, the whole figure rotates 60 degrees clockwise. The grey droplet alternates between being on top of and behind the hatched triangle. The black rectangle alternates between being behind the droplet on the right, in front of the droplet in the middle and behind the droplet on the left.

**7) D**

Going in a clockwise direction from the top hexagon, each line with a circle on the end moves down one place, with the line at the bottom moving to the top. One more triangle is shaded in, moving from top to bottom. Once all the triangles are shaded, one more triangle is shaded white each time, moving from top to bottom. The rectangle and triangles alternate between grey and black shading.

**8) B**

Going in a clockwise direction from the top hexagon, the top shape in each hexagon is rotated 90 degrees clockwise to become the bottom shape in the next hexagon. The shading of the circles goes in the order: black, black, grey, grey, white, white.

## Pages 14-15 — Changing Bugs

**1) B**

Each shading on the bug's wings moves one place clockwise to the next part of the wing. Copies of the top shape inside the bug's body appear on the ends of the antennae, and the top shape inside the bug's body disappears.

**2) C**

The two legs at the top of the bug's body move in front of the bug's body. The bug's eyes take on the shading of the bug's feet, matching the order of the shading from left to right.

**3) C**

The bug's legs and head reflect downwards. Half of the bug's body is shaded white.

**4) A**

The top shape in the bug's body rotates 45 degrees anticlockwise to become the left-hand wing. The bottom shape in the bug's body rotates 45 degrees clockwise to become the right-hand wing. The two shapes inside the bug's body swap shadings. The bug's eyes move apart.

**5) D**

The two shapes inside the bug's body swap positions. Black shapes at the top of the bug become white and white shapes become black. An extra line is added at a right angle to each of the bug's legs.

**6) A**

The top two shapes in the bug's body swap shadings and the bottom two shapes swap shadings. The middle shape in the bug's body rotates 90 degrees clockwise. The wings take on the line type of the antennae.

**7) B**

One shape is added to the left-hand side of the bug's body and one shape is removed from the right-hand side. The bug's head gains a side. Each shading on the bug's legs moves to the next leg in a clockwise direction.

**8) D**

The shape inside the bug's body at the bottom gets bigger, turns white and becomes the bug's head. The shapes in the top two corners get bigger and take on the shading of the shape inside the bug's body at the bottom to become the bug's wings. The shape of the bug's legs becomes the shape of the bug's antennae, and the bug's legs disappear.

**9) C**

The shape of the bug's head swaps with the shape of the bug's body. The shape inside the bug's head is reflected across to become the shapes on the ends of the bug's antennae, and the shape inside the bug's head disappears. The number of shapes inside the bug's body becomes the number of legs.

**10) D**

The number of shapes on the ends of the bug's antennae becomes the number of segments inside the bug's body. The shading of the segments starting at the top left segment and moving clockwise matches the shading of the antennae shapes moving left to right. The shape of the bug's feet becomes the shape of the bug's head. The arms swap line types.

## Rotation and Reflection

### Pages 16-17 — Rotate the Figure

**1) D**

The figure is rotated 45 degrees anticlockwise. Option A is a reflection. Option B has an extra section of the shape shaded grey. Option C is missing a section of grey shading.

**2) C**

The figure is rotated 135 degrees clockwise. In options A and D, the wrong heart is shaded black. In option B, the shape in the centre of the triangle is a pentagon instead of a hexagon.

**3) B**

The figure is rotated 45 degrees clockwise. In option A, the square and the circle have swapped places. Option C is a reflection. In option D, the circle is in the wrong position.

**4) D**

The figure is rotated 90 degrees clockwise. In option A, the dots have swapped shading. Option B is a reflection. In option C, the grey dot is in the wrong position.

**5) A**

The figure is rotated 180 degrees. In option B, the wavy line is upside down. Option C is a rotated reflection. In option D, the black arrow is pointing in the wrong direction.

**6) C**

The figure is rotated 180 degrees. In option A, the hexagon is rotated incorrectly. In option B, the hexagon and the triangle have swapped places. In option D, the shapes are in the wrong corners of the squares.

**7) D**

The figure is rotated 90 degrees anticlockwise. In option A, the small four-sided shape has been reflected. In option B, the wrong line is dashed. Option C is a rotated reflection.

**8) B**

The figure is rotated 135 degrees anticlockwise. In option A, the lines are too far apart. In option C, the wrong square is shaded grey. Option D is a rotated reflection.

**9) C**

The figure is rotated 135 degrees anticlockwise. In option A, the white circle sector is rotated incorrectly. Option B is a rotated reflection. In option D, the black circle sector is rotated incorrectly.

**10) D**

The figure is rotated 90 degrees anticlockwise. Option A is a rotated reflection. Option B is a reflection. In option C, the shading is incorrect.

## Pages 18-19 — Reflect the Figure

**1) C**

Option A is a 180 degree rotation. Option B is missing part of the line. Option D is a 90 degree clockwise rotation.

**2) B**

In option A, the two arrows have not been reflected. Option C is a 180 degree rotation. In option D, the arrowhead is on the wrong end of the dashed arrow.

**3) A**

In option B, the diagonal lines have not been reflected. In option C, the grey and white circles to the left of the figure have swapped places. In option D, the black and white circles at the bottom of the figure have swapped places.

**4) D**

In option A, the star at the bottom has been rotated. In option B, the triangle in the middle row has been reflected downwards. In option C, the triangle in the top row has not been reflected.

**5) B**

In option A, the hatching has not been reflected. In option C, the hatching has been reflected but the shape has been rotated 180 degrees. In option D, the hatching has been reflected but the shape is a 135 degree clockwise rotation.

**6) C**

In option A, one of the small vertical lines is in the wrong place. Option B is a reflection. In option D, the black and grey triangles in the centre have the wrong shading.

**7) B**

Option A is a 180 degree rotation. Option C is a 90 degree clockwise rotation with the grey and black shading swapped. Option D is a rotated reflection.

**8) D**

In option A, the top L-shape has not been reflected. Option B is a 180 degree rotation. In option C, the left and right L-shapes are in the wrong positions.

**9) D**

Option A has been reflected downwards. In option B, the grey shapes aren't linked with the white shapes. In option C, the bottom white shape isn't linked to the others.

**10) C**

Options A and B have the wrong shape. In option D, the figure has been reflected downwards.

# Spatial Reasoning

## Pages 20-21 — 3D Rotation

**1) C**

Shape C has been rotated 90 degrees anticlockwise in the plane of the page. It has then been rotated 180 degrees towards you, top-to-bottom.

**2) A**

Shape A has been rotated 90 degrees anticlockwise in the plane of the page. It has then been rotated 180 degrees left-to-right.

**3) D**

Shape D has been rotated 180 degrees in the plane of the page. It has then been rotated 90 degrees left-to-right.

**4) B**

Shape B has been rotated 90 degrees clockwise in the plane of the page. It has then been rotated 90 degrees right-to-left.

**5) F**

Shape F has been rotated 90 degrees anticlockwise in the plane of the page. It has then been rotated 90 degrees right-to-left.

**6) D**

Shape D has been rotated 90 degrees towards you, top-to-bottom. It has then been rotated 90 degrees anticlockwise in the plane of the page.

**7) C**

Shape C has been rotated 90 degrees away from you, top-to-bottom. It has then been rotated 90 degrees anticlockwise in the plane of the page.

**8) E**

Shape E has been rotated 90 degrees clockwise in the plane of the page. It has then been rotated 90 degrees right-to-left.

**9) B**

Shape B has been rotated 180 degrees in the plane of the page. It has then between rotated 90 degrees away from you, top-to-bottom.

**10) A**

Shape A has been rotated 90 degrees anticlockwise in the plane of the page. It has then been rotated 90 degrees away from you, top-to-bottom.

## Pages 22-23 — 3D Building Blocks

**1) A**

The top block of A rotates 90 degrees right-to-left and is at the front of the figure. The block at the bottom of A is arranged underneath it. The middle block of A rotates 90 degrees in the plane of the page and is at the back of the figure.

**2) D**

The bottom block of D rotates 90 degrees clockwise in the plane of the page and is at the back of the figure. The top left block of D rotates 90 degrees anticlockwise in the plane of the page and is arranged in front of it. The top right block of D is arranged at the top right of the figure.

**3) C**

The top right block of C is at the front of the figure. The bottom left block of C is arranged behind it. The bottom right block of C rotates 90 degrees left-to-right. It then rotates 90 degrees towards you, top-to-bottom, and is arranged on the right-hand side of the figure.

**4) B**

The top block of B rotates 90 degrees left-to-right and is arranged on the left-hand side of the figure. The bottom left block of B rotates 90 degrees in the plane of the page and is arranged in the middle of the figure. The bottom right block of B rotates 90 degrees anticlockwise in the plane of the page. It is then rotates 90 degrees away from you, top-to-bottom, and is arranged at the back of the figure.

**5) C**

The top left block of C is in the middle of the figure. The top right block of C rotates 90 degrees clockwise in the plane of the page. It then rotates 90 degrees towards you, top-to-bottom, and is arranged at the bottom of the figure. The bottom block of C is above it.

**6) B**

The bottom block of B rotates 90 degrees clockwise in the plane of the page and is on the left-hand side of the figure. The top right block of B rotates 90 degrees right-to-left and is arranged to the right of it. The top left block of B rotates 90 degrees away from you, top-to-bottom, and is on the right-hand side of the figure.

**7) A**

The top block of A rotates 90 degrees away from you, top-to-bottom, and is arranged at the front of the figure. The bottom left block of A is arranged at the back of the figure. The bottom right block of A rotates 90 degrees away from you, top-to-bottom, and is arranged at the top right of the figure.

**8) D**

The top right block of D is at the front of the figure. The top left block of D rotates 90 degrees clockwise in the plane of the page and is arranged in the middle of the figure. The bottom block of D rotates 90 degrees anticlockwise in the plane of the page. It then rotates 90 degrees left-to-right and is arranged at the back of the figure.

**9) C**

The bottom block of C rotates 180 degrees in the plane of the page and is at the back of the figure. The top right block of C rotates 90 degrees right-to-left and is arranged on the left of the figure. The top left block of C is at the front of the figure.

## Pages 24-25 — 2D Views of 3D Shapes

**1) B**

There are seven blocks visible from above, which rules out options C and D. There are three blocks in the middle row, which rules out option A.

**2) D**

There are seven blocks visible from above, which rules out option C. The figure is made up of three rows of blocks, which rules out option A. There is one block visible on the left-hand side, which rules out option B.

**3) C**

There are eight blocks visible from above, which rules out option A. There are three blocks visible at the front, which rules out option D. There are two blocks visible at the back, which rules out option B.

**4) A**

There are seven blocks visible from above, which rules out option B. There are two blocks visible at the back, which rules out option C. There is one block visible at the front, which rules out option D.

**5) A**

There are seven blocks visible from above, which rules out option D. There is one block visible at the back, which rules out options B and C.

**6) B**

There are three blocks visible on the right-hand side, which rules out options C and D. There is one block visible at the front, which rules out option A.

**7) D**

There are seven blocks visible from above, which rules out option B. There are two blocks visible at the back, which rules out options A and C.

**8) C**

There is one block visible at the back, which rules out options A and B. There are three blocks visible on the left-hand side, which rules out option D.

**9) C**

There are three blocks visible at the back, which rules out options A and B. There is one block visible at the front, which rules out option D.

## Pages 26-27 — Cubes and Nets

**1) C**

Option A is ruled out because the grey hexagon and the black and white square must be on opposite sides. Option B is ruled out because the grey and white five-sided shape has been reflected. Option D is ruled out because if the hatching is at the top and the grey and white five-sided shape is at the front, then the black and white square must be on the right.

**2) B**

Option A is ruled out because the black circle over the X-shape must be opposite the white and black stars. Option C is ruled out because if a grey triangle is at the top, pointing to the top left, and the black circle over the X-shape is on the right, then the white circle on the black square must be at the front. Option D is ruled out because the grey triangle should be pointing to the top right corner.

**3) D**

Option A is ruled out because the face with the X-shape has been rotated. Option B is ruled out because the circles and the X-shape must be on opposite sides. Option C is ruled out because the white star and the spiral must be on opposite sides.

**4) A**

Option B is ruled out because the four arrowheads have been rotated. Option C is ruled out because the black circle and white square have been rotated. Option D is ruled out because if the two ovals are at the top and the black rectangles are at the front, then the black circle and white square should be on the right.

**5) C**

Option A is ruled out because the grey semicircle shapes have been rotated. Option B is ruled out because the triangle with the thick outline has been rotated. Option D is ruled out because the triangle with the thick outline and the grey face with the white star must be on opposite sides.

**6) C**

Option A is ruled out because the face on the right has been rotated. Option B is ruled out because the face at the front has been reflected across. Option D is ruled out because the face on the right should be the face with four dots in the corners.

**7) D**

Option A is ruled out because the grey circle with a line through it has been rotated. Option B is ruled out because the face with the grey rectangle has been rotated. Option C is ruled out because the face with the grey and black semicircles has been reflected downwards.

**8) A**

Options B and C are ruled out because the face at the top has been rotated. Option D is ruled out because the left-hand side of the face at the front should be shaded white.

## Pages 28-29 — Fold Along the Line

**1) A**

Options B and D are ruled out because the part of the figure originally to the left of the fold line is the wrong shape. Option C is ruled out because the part of the figure that has been folded is the wrong shape.

**2) A**

Option B is ruled out because the fold line has moved. Option C is ruled out because the figure has been broken apart along the fold line. Option D is ruled out because the part of the figure that has been folded is the wrong shape.

**3) B**

Option A is ruled out because the fold line has moved. Option C is ruled out because the part of the figure originally below the fold line is the wrong shape. Option D is ruled out because the part of the figure that has been folded is the wrong shape.

**4) C**

Option A is ruled out because the part of the figure originally below the fold line is the wrong shape. Option B is ruled out because the part of the figure that has been folded is the wrong shape. Option D is ruled out because the fold line has moved.

**5) D**

Option A is ruled out because a part of the figure that was originally above the fold line is missing. Option B is ruled out because the part of the figure that has been folded is the wrong shape. Option C is ruled out because the part of the figure originally above the fold line should still be visible.

**6) B**

Options A and C are ruled out because the fold line has moved. Option D is ruled out because the part of the figure that has been folded is the wrong shape.

**7) C**

Option A is ruled out because the fold line has moved. Option B is ruled out because the part of the figure that has been folded is the wrong shape. Option D is ruled out because the part of the figure originally above the fold line is the wrong shape.

**8) A**

Option B is ruled out because the part of the figure that has been folded is the wrong shape. Option C is ruled out because the fold line has moved. Option D is ruled out because the part of the figure originally above the fold line is the wrong shape.

**9) D**

Option A is ruled out because the part of the figure originally below the fold line is the wrong shape. Option B is ruled out because the part of the figure that has been folded is the wrong shape. Option C is ruled out because the fold line has moved.

**10) B**

Options A and C are ruled out because the part of the figure that has been folded is the wrong shape. Option D is ruled out because the part of the figure originally above the fold line is the wrong shape.

**11) C**

Options A and D are ruled out because the part of the figure that has been folded is the wrong shape. Option B is ruled out because the part of the figure originally below the fold line is the wrong shape.

## Pages 30-31 — Fold and Punch

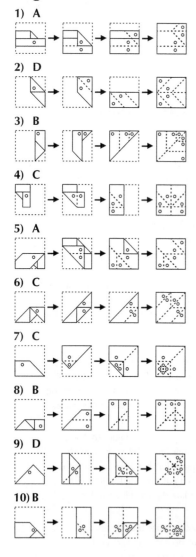

**1) A**

**2) D**

**3) B**

**4) C**

**5) A**

**6) C**

**7) C**

**8) B**

**9) D**

**10) B**

## Pages 32-41 — Assessment Test 1

### Section 1 — Find the Figure Like the First Two

**1) D**

All figures are made from three overlapping shapes. Two of the shapes are identical apart from size, and the third is different.

**2) D**

In all figures, starting from the longest line and going anticlockwise around the circle, the lines get shorter in length. Starting from the smallest sector and going anticlockwise around the circle, the sectors get larger in area.

**3) A**

In all figures, all four-sided regions are shaded grey.

**4) B**

In all figures, the shading of the upper half of the top shape matches the shading of the lower half of the middle shape, the shading of the lower half of the top shape matches the shading of the upper half of the bottom shape, and the shading of the upper half of the middle shape matches the shading of the lower half of the bottom shape.

**5) C**

In all figures, four short lines go through four different sides of the large shape. A short line goes through the centre of a side only when the circles at its ends have matching shading.

**6) B**

In all figures, the white circles are positioned so it looks like they are on the corners of a shape (e.g. square, hexagon, octagon). Arrows on opposite 'corners' have the same arrowhead and point in opposite directions.

**7) C**

In all figures, the arrows can be arranged head to tail to form the outline of the white shape.

**8) B**

In all figures, the circle has two solid arcs and one dashed arc. The number of dotted arcs is equal to the number of hexagons inside the circle.

**9) A**

In all figures, there are two grey circles. The circles beneath the black shape are layered front to back. The number of white circles layered beneath the black shape is equal to its number of sides.

### Section 2 — Rotate the Figure

**1) D**

The figure has been rotated 90 degrees clockwise. In option A, the white oval has the wrong rotation. Option B is a rotated reflection. In option C, the grey oval has the wrong rotation.

**2) D**

The figure has been rotated 180 degrees. Option A is a rotated reflection. Option B is a downwards reflection. Option C has been reflected across.

**3) B**

The figure has been rotated 90 degrees clockwise. Option A is a rotated reflection. In option C, the two middle circles have swapped places. Option D has been reflected across.

**4) B**

The figure has been rotated 180 degrees. In option A, the black dots on the points of the star are in the wrong positions. Option C is a downwards reflection. Option D is a rotated reflection.

**5) D**

The figure has been rotated 135 degrees anticlockwise. In option A, the circle and square have swapped places. In option B, the square has the wrong rotation. Option C is a rotated reflection.

**6) C**

The figure is rotated 180 degrees. Option A is a rotated reflection. In option B, the outer two of the shorter lines have swapped places. In option D, the two longer lines are a rotated reflection.

**7) A**

The figure has been rotated 135 degrees clockwise.
Options B and C are rotated reflections. In option D,
the small black triangles have the wrong rotation.

**8) C**

The figure has been rotated 135 degrees clockwise.
Option A is the wrong shape. Option B is a rotated reflection.
In option D, the wrong hexagons are shaded grey.

**9) A**

The figure is rotated 45 degrees anticlockwise. Option B is a
reflection. In option C, the grey shapes have not been rotated.
In option D, the hatchings have the wrong rotations.

**10) B**

The figure is rotated 90 degrees clockwise.
In options A and D, the lines inside the circles have
the wrong rotation. Option C is a rotated reflection.

## Section 3 — Complete the Pair

**1) C**

The largest overlap of the shapes is shaded black, then
rotated 180 degrees. The original shapes are removed.

**2) A**

Starting with the black star at the top, the stars are joined
in the order: black, grey, white, black, grey, white.

**3) D**

The hatchings of the circles move one place anticlockwise
around the circles. The shadings of the triangles move one place
downwards, with the bottom shading moving to the top.

**4) A**

The white shapes swap places, then the
shadings move one place clockwise.

**5) C**

The whole figure is reflected downwards, then the
dashed and dotted lines swap size and position.

**6) A**

The figure is rotated 90 degrees clockwise, then the grey
shadings move to the bottom of each column. If the shadings
are already at the bottom, then they stay where they are.

**7) B**

The shadings of the dots becomes grey, except for the pair of dots
that could be connected by a line in the direction of the hatching
in the large shape — the shading of those two dots is swapped.

**8) C**

The shapes are layered in the order of the lengths of the arrows
around them, so that the shape with the longest arrow is at the
back. Each shape gets smaller if its arrow goes clockwise and
larger if its arrow goes anticlockwise. All arrows are removed.

## Section 4 — Cubes and Nets

**1) B**

Option A is ruled out because the face with the black and
white circles has been rotated. Option C is ruled out because
if the black oval is at the front and the hatched square is on
the top, then the black and white triangles must be on the
right. Option D is ruled out because the black oval and
the grey and white chevrons must be on opposite sides.

**2) B**

Option A is ruled out because if the hatched square is on
the top and the grey and black arches are at the front, then
the black droplet must be on the right. Option C is ruled
out because the three lines have been reflected. Option D
is ruled out because the black droplet has been rotated.

**3) D**

Option A is ruled out because the grey shape with two sloping
sides and the five-pointed star must be on opposite sides. Option B
is ruled out because if the black circle with white hatching is at
the front and the six-pointed star is at the top, then the grey
shape with two sloping sides must be on the right. Option C
is ruled out because if the black diamond with white hatching
is at the front and the grey square with a corner missing is on
the top, then the other grey shape must be on the right.

**4) D**

Option A is ruled out because the curved grey shape and the four
triangles must be on opposite sides. Option B is ruled out because if
the black hexagon is at the top and the grey circle and white pentagon
are on the right, then the curved grey shape must be at the front.
Option C is ruled out because the four triangles have been rotated.

**5) A**

Option B is ruled out because the white square and grey triangle have
been rotated. Option C is ruled out because if the white and grey
rings are at the front and the curved line is on the right, then the three
white rectangles must be on the top. Option D is ruled out because
the face with the white circles and zigzag line has been reflected.

**6) D**

Option A is ruled out because the face with the black and white circles
has been rotated. Option B is ruled out because if the two four-sided
grey shapes are at the front and the black and white circles are on the
top, then the black square must be on the right. Option C is ruled
out because if the black stars are at the front and the two grey arches
are at the top, then the black and white circles must be on the right.

**7) B**

Option A is ruled out because the face with the four triangles has
been reflected. Option C is ruled out because if the spiral is at the
top and the grey triangle is on the right, then the four triangles
must be at the front. Option D is ruled out because if the black
circle and the white arch are at the front and the white and grey
rectangles are on the right, then the spiral must be on the top.

**8) C**

Option A is ruled out because the diagonal line on the top face is in
the wrong place. Option B is ruled out because if the top and right
faces are correct then the wrong face is at the front, or else if the
top and front faces are correct then the wrong face is on the right.
Option D is ruled out because the face at the top has been rotated.

## Section 5 — Fold and Punch

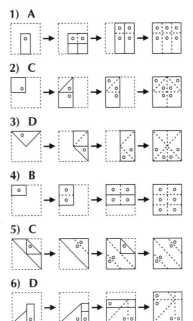

**1) A**

**2) C**

**3) D**

**4) B**

**5) C**

**6) D**

**7) C**

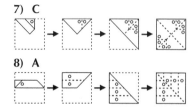

**8) A**

# Pages 42-51 — Assessment Test 2

## Section 1 — Complete the Square Grid

**1) B**
Working from left to right, the rectangle moves to the next side of the grid square, moving in a clockwise direction. The rectangles in each row have the same shading. One more shaded circle is added, alternating between white and black.

**2) C**
Working from left to right, the whole figure rotates 90 degrees anticlockwise. The shape at the front moves to the back and the shape at the back moves to the front.

**3) A**
Working from left to right, the large shape reflects across to the next grid square. Each line moves to the next corner, moving in an anticlockwise direction around the grid square.

**4) C**
In each row, the shape in the right-hand grid square is made up of the bottom right-hand quarter of the shape in the left-hand grid square and the shading of the largest circle in the middle grid square.

**5) D**
There are semicircles in every corner of the central grid square, and every corner that touches it. The semicircles alternate between grey and black. Each shape only appears once in each row and column. Each shape is positioned at the top of the grid square, in the middle and at the bottom.

**6) B**
Working from left to right, the arrow moves to point to the next shortest shape. Each shading moves one place to the right, with the shading on the right-hand side moving to the left-hand side. Each type of arrowhead appears only once in each row and column.

**7) D**
Working from left to right, the number of lines that make up the outline of the square increases by one. One more gap appears in the outline of the square. Another line is added to the centre of the square, at a 45 degree clockwise rotation to the previous line. The circle moves one place anticlockwise around the corners of the square.

## Section 2 — Odd One Out

**1) D**
In all other figures, the white shape on the top is a smaller, 90 degree clockwise rotation of the white shape at the bottom.

**2) D**
In all other figures, the number of lines inside the white shape is equal to its number of sides.

**3) B**
In all other figures, there must be an equal number of cross-shapes and clockwise arrows.

**4) A**
In all other figures, the dotted line is next to a circle that has the same shading as most of the circles in the figure.

**5) B**
In all other figures, the black raindrop is inside a five-sided shape.

**6) E**
In all other figures, the white circle is the closest circle to the point where the two lines overlap.

**7) C**
In all other figures, the top shape, when reflected across, matches the part of the bottom shape that isn't overlapped by the curved shape.

**8) A**
In all other figures, the shading of the shape the arrow is pointing to is the same as the shading of the highest shape connected to the outer line.

**9) D**
In all other figures, the number of circles matches the number of sides of the shape made by the overlap of the two large white shapes.

## Section 3 — Complete the Series

**1) B**
In each series square, the whole figure rotates 90 degrees clockwise. Each shading moves one place to the next largest circle. When a shading reaches the largest circle, it moves back to the smallest circle.

**2) A**
In each series square, the whole figure rotates 90 degrees clockwise and the grey and black shadings swap.

**3) D**
In each series square, each triangle moves one place to the left, but the shadings don't move. The left-hand triangle moves to the right-hand side. The semicircle moves one place to the left and rotates 90 degrees anticlockwise.

**4) C**
In each series square, the whole figure rotates 45 degrees clockwise. The grey shape increases in size in the direction of the remaining white shape in the last figure. One white shape disappears, moving in a clockwise direction around the figure.

**5) A**
In each series square, a new triangle is added. One oval disappears and the new triangle takes on the shading of the oval that is now on the left-hand side. The other triangles each reflect downwards.

**6) B**
The squares in this series are in two pairs. In each pair, the two large white shapes swap layering. Each grey circle moves to the opposite side of the white shape it is on. Each arrow moves to point in the opposite direction.

**7) C**
In each series square, the white square and the white and black triangles rotate together 90 degrees clockwise. The black and white triangles swap shadings. The small white and grey shape rotates 90 degrees anticlockwise and the shadings swap.

**8) C**
In each series square, the black shading moves one place down. The grey shading moves one place to the left. One more corner square is removed, moving in a clockwise direction around the corners.

**9) D**
The top small shape becomes the large shape in the next series square (the large shape is always white). The bottom small shape moves to the top in the next series square. A new small shape appears at the bottom, that alternates between white and grey.

## Section 4 — 3D Rotation

**1) F**
Shape F rotates 90 degrees anticlockwise in the plane of the page, then 90 degrees left-to-right.

**2) D**
Shape D rotates 90 degrees away from you, top-to-bottom, then 90 degrees left-to-right.

**3) A**
Shape A rotates 90 degrees towards you, top-to-bottom, then 90 degrees right-to-left.

**4) C**

Shape C rotates 180 degrees right-to-left.

**5) D**

Shape D is rotated 180 degrees in the plane of the page.

**6) E**

Shape E rotates 90 degrees left-to-right, then 90 degrees away from you, top-to-bottom.

**7) C**

Shape C rotates 90 degrees towards you, top-to-bottom, then 90 degrees right-to-left.

**8) A**

Shape A rotates 90 degrees away from you top-to-bottom, then 90 degrees right-to-left.

**9) F**

Shape F rotates 90 degrees clockwise in the plane of the page, then 90 degrees left-to-right.

**10) B**

Shape B rotates 90 degrees towards you, top-to-bottom, then 90 degrees left-to-right.

## Section 5 — 2D Views of 3D Shapes

**1) C**

There are seven blocks visible from above, which rules out options A and B. There are three blocks visible on the right-hand side, which rules out option D.

**2) A**

There are five blocks visible from above, which rules out options B and D. There are three rows of blocks, which rules out option C.

**3) D**

There are six blocks visible from above, which rules out options A and B. There is one block visible on the right-hand side, which rules out option C.

**4) A**

There are seven blocks visible from above, which rules out options B and D. There is a gap between the two blocks on the left-hand side, which rules out option C.

**5) B**

There are three blocks visible on the left-hand side, which rules out options A and C. There are four blocks visible on the right-hand side, which rules out option D.

**6) B**

There is one block visible at the front, which rules out option A. There are three blocks visible on the right-hand side, which rules out option C. There are at least two blocks visible on the left-hand side, which rules out option D.

**7) D**

There are three blocks visible on the left-hand side, which rules out options A and C. There are two blocks visible at the front, which rules out option B.

**8) C**

There are seven blocks visible from above, which rules out options A and B. There is one block visible at the back, which rules out option D.

# Pages 52-61 — Assessment Test 3

## Section 1 — Reflect the Figure

**1) D**

In option A, the triangle hasn't been reflected.
In option B, the black and grey shapes have swapped layering.
In option C, the white shape has been rotated.

**2) B**

In option A, the white shapes are the wrong shapes.
In option C, the grey and black shapes are the wrong shapes.
In option D, the top of the grey shape is the wrong shape.

**3) A**

In option B, the black triangle has been rotated.
In option C, the diagonal line hasn't been reflected.
In option D, the black and grey shadings in the curved shapes have swapped.

**4) A**

In option B, the circle sector has been rotated, not reflected.
In option C, the grey strip is in the wrong place.
In option D, the zig-zag lines are the wrong shape.

**5) C**

In option A, the two lines at the top of the large white shape are in the wrong place. Option B is a rotation. In option D, the right-hand half of the large white shape is the wrong shape.

**6) D**

In option A, the grey shape is the wrong shape. In option B, the curved cut-out on the top-right of the white shape is the wrong shape. In option C, the curved cut-out on the bottom-left of the white shape is the wrong shape.

**7) C**

In option A, the thin lines with the grey and white shapes have been reflected but the thick black lines have been rotated. In option B, the grey shape hasn't been reflected. In option D, the thick black lines have been reflected but the thin lines with the white and grey shapes haven't.

**8) B**

In option A, the middle white and grey shapes are the wrong shapes. In option C, the left-hand grey shape is the wrong shape. In option D, the right-hand white shape is the wrong shape.

**9) D**

In option A, the two short lines connected together on the top right have swapped positions. In option B, the hatching hasn't been reflected. In option C, the short black line on the end of the curved line has the wrong rotation.

## Section 2 — Fold Along the Line

**1) D**

Option A is ruled out because the fold line has moved. Options B and C are ruled out because the part of the figure that has been folded is the wrong shape.

**2) C**

Option A is ruled out because the part of the figure originally to the right of the fold line should still be visible. Options B and D are ruled out because the part of the figure that has been folded is the wrong shape.

**3) A**

Options B, C and D are ruled out because the part of the figure that has been folded is the wrong shape.

**4) B**

Option A is ruled out because the part of the figure originally to the right of the fold line is the wrong shape. Option C is ruled out because the part of the figure that has been folded is the wrong shape. Option D is ruled out because the fold line has moved.

**5) A**

Option B is ruled out because the part of the figure that has been folded is the wrong shape. Option C is ruled out because the part of the figure originally above the fold line is the wrong shape. Option D is ruled out because the fold line has moved.

**6) D**

Option A is ruled out because the fold line has moved. Option B is ruled out because the part of the figure that has been folded is the wrong shape. Option C is ruled out because the part of the figure originally to the right of the fold line is the wrong shape.

**7) B**

Option A is ruled out because the part of the figure originally to the right of the fold line is the wrong shape. Option C is ruled out because the part of the figure that has been folded is the wrong shape. Option D is ruled out because the fold line has moved.

**8) C**

Option A is ruled out because the part of the figure that has been folded is the wrong shape. Option B is ruled out because the part of the figure originally to the left of the fold line is the wrong shape. Option D is ruled out because the fold line has moved.

## Section 3 — Complete the Hexagonal Grid

**1) D**

Going in a clockwise direction, each outer hexagon rotates 60 degrees clockwise.

**2) B**

Going in a clockwise direction from the top hexagon, the next largest four-sided shape is shaded in grey. The black and white triangles swap shadings.

**3) C**

Going in an anticlockwise direction from the top hexagon, each hexagon rotates 60 degrees anticlockwise. The circle moves further along the line, towards the centre of the hexagonal grid.

**4) D**

Going in a clockwise direction from the top hexagon, the figure rotates 90 degrees clockwise and one more rectangle is added, connected by one of its shortest sides to the previously added rectangle. The shading of new rectangles alternates between white and black.

**5) A**

Going in an anticlockwise direction, the direction of the arrow and the shading of the circle match the direction and shading of the raindrop in the next hexagon.

**6) C**

Going in an anticlockwise direction from the top-left hexagon, one more semicircle line is added to the spiral and the spiral reflects across. The triangle gets smaller and reflects across.

**7) B**

The hexagons on opposite sides of the hexagonal grid are in pairs. The large shapes in the middle of the first three hexagons, going in a clockwise direction from the top hexagon, lose their right-hand halves and rotate 90 degrees clockwise, to become the middle shapes in the opposite hexagons. The middle shapes and the triangles at the bottom of each hexagon swap shadings within these pairs.

**8) D**

Going in a clockwise direction from the top hexagon, one white shape is removed, alternating between a square and a circle. One more cross is added to the place where the white shape was removed from, alternating between a 'x' shape and a '+' shape.

## Section 4 — Changing Bugs

**1) D**

The shadings in the bug's head swap. The bug's legs take on the shape inside the bug's body and the shape inside the bug's body disappears. The shape of the original legs becomes the shape of the antennae.

**2) C**

The top half of the bug's head disappears. Each circle inside the bug's body moves one place clockwise to the next line.

**3) A**

A portion of the bug's head is cut away, in the shape of the shape inside the bug's body. The shape inside the bug's body reflects downwards. The shapes on the ends of the bug's antennae become the bug's legs — these shapes aren't rotated.

**4) B**

The number of line segments inside the bug's body becomes the number of legs. An extra side is added to the bug's head. The bug's head takes on the shading of the shape in the corner of the bug's body.

**5) A**

The top two and the bottom two legs reflect downwards. The top circle rotates 180 degrees, the second circle down rotates 90 degrees clockwise, the third circle down rotates 45 degrees clockwise and the bottom circle rotates 90 degrees anticlockwise.

**6) C**

The bug's wings and the circles reflect upwards. A number of line shapes appear on the bug's body, which matches the number of circles on each wing.

**7) D**

Each shading on the bug's wings moves to the next outer section of the wing. The shading of the outermost section moves to the innermost section. The two outer shapes on the ends of the lines at the bottom of the bug swap places. Copies of the new right-hand shape move to the ends of the antennae. The middle shape at the bottom is rotated 90 degrees.

**8) A**

Each of the bug's legs moves down one place, with the bottom leg moving to the top. A copy of the bug's head that has been rotated 90 degrees anticlockwise is placed inside the bug's body. Eyes that are at the back of the bug's head move to the front and eyes that are at the front move to the back.

**9) D**

The bug's legs reflect across. The top two legs take on the top shading inside the bug's body, the two middle legs take on the middle shading inside the bug's body and the two bottom legs take on the bottom shading inside the bug's body. The shape inside the bug's body becomes the shape of the bug's head.

**10) B**

The bug's top-left wing rotates 45 degrees anticlockwise and the bug's top-right wing rotates 45 degrees clockwise. Each wing moves to the centre of the bug's body. The line shape inside the bug's body reflects across. The circles on the ends of the antennae take on the shading of the top shape at the bottom of the bug's body.

## Section 5 — 3D Building Blocks

**1) A**

The block at the top of set A rotates 180 degrees right-to-left, then 90 degrees clockwise in the plane of the page to become the block at the back of the figure. The block at the bottom of set A rotates 90 degrees in the plane of the page to become the block on the right. The block on the left of set A rotates 90 degrees towards you, top-to-bottom, then 90 degrees right-to-left to become the remaining block.

**2) A**

The block at the top of set A rotates 90 degrees anticlockwise in the plane of the page, then 90 degrees left-to-right to become the block at the front of the figure. The block on the bottom right of set A rotates 90 degrees clockwise in the plane of the page to become the block at the back of the figure, at the bottom. The block at the bottom left of set A rotates 90 degrees in the plane of the page to become the block at the back of the figure, at the top.

**3) B**

The block at the top of set B rotates 90 degrees away from you, top-to-bottom, to become the bottom block in the figure. The remaining two blocks in set B are arranged on the left of the figure and at the top.

**4) C**

The two cubes in set C go at the back of the figure on the left-hand side and the right-hand side. The block at the top of set C rotates 90 degrees right-to-left, then 90 degrees towards you, top-to-bottom, and then moves between the two cubes. The remaining block in set C is at the front of the figure.